Blessing of the Chains

Deneithia Jackson

ISBN 979-8-89043-168-4 (paperback)
ISBN 979-8-89043-169-1 (digital)

Christian Faith Publishing
832 Park Avenue
Meadville, PA 16335
www.christianfaithpublishing.com

Printed in the United States of America

In loving memories,
Betty Jean Jackson, a great history storyteller!
December 2, 1935–December 18, 2020

Introduction

When hearing all about wisdom in history books, about how certain people's descendant ancestors learn or do certain things that stand out in the history books. Still there was no successful conclusion until years down the line! But what if history books missed one beautiful story that no one dares to talk about, a group of slaves that got away and never to be found with the help of an old, white witch? Now life, as we know it, can have a blessing and a curse in the setting. But once you get control, the road to success will become everlasting! This is my story about a group of slaves taking a risk of trusting a stranger that just might take up their lives in danger to reach freedom. They were not aware of the magical life on maypop mountain that they were unprepared for!

The Plantation

This story starts with living on a sugar plantation farm about fifteen miles on the outskirts of the northern coast of the Carolina Mountains. This plantation was always a topic of discussion in the local communities for many reasons. The reason for such talk from the townspeople is the cause, this sugar plantation was once owned by a wealthy white man (Mr. Health), known for his high-quality sugar cane! Mr. Health Jr. came from a long generation of men of wealth from the sugar farm, as well as their healthy group of slaves there on the plantation. Mr. Health Sr. was a man of order and image when out in the public's eye! But back home, he was a very spiritual man. They enjoyed his slaves singing in such a manner while taking diligent care of the plantation's chores. He (Mr. Heath, sir) very rarely must raise his voice to them so that it would harm one of them (slaves)! Mr. Health believed in great details of how a happy slave produces enormous wealth in the crop and a well-kept land keeps the illness away as the sun shines high and bright as a gift from God, for horning his word of giving thanks to his land and his people.

Whenever Mr. Health must go to the town for supplies, he would have to take on the role of a nasty slave owner. The universally loved slave owner would prepare himself by adding wrinkles to his head, his nose up in the air as far as he could while placing chewing tobacco in the right corner of his jaw! He would tell his slaves to look sad and all eyes on the ground as they enter the town's welcoming bridge! As Mr. Health would enter the general store for supplies, he would always feel the eyes staring at his back, as if they knew his secrets of how he kept his crops and slaves away. The other owner would dare to run the risk of hanging for the sake of loving on his slaves. Mr. Health never had to worry about his people running away, stealing his crops to eat, or doing anything to harm his wife and children as they lived together on the healthy sugar plantation.

One special night, Mr. Health allowed them to sing and dance in the back of his home as he watched, sitting on his back porch while rocking in his locker, smoking his granddad's pipe. Even though he made a massive amount of money from the medicine that the slaves made in their homes, they loved him so much! The medicine lady would come down (from the high end of the forest) to his home and cover him with health and blessings to end his journey as an old man who would die of natural causes. Did such that at the age of ninety-seven years old, Mr. Health's life was cut when the wagon that he was riding lost one wheel, and he fell and broke his neck. That day was the first day the sun's head bowed, as tears began to fall while the sun did not switch out with the clouds. Now Mr. Health's slaves must prepare the plantation for its new owner. With their hearts still heavy, some walk around the ground still weeping, as if the accident happened yesterday! The town's mayor ordered the slaves to be locked in one servant's quarter to be prepared for sale in the town's auction within three days! That gave the town's mayor the chance to place more money into the city's hands at the expense of the healthy sugar plantation. This did not sit well with the slaves at all as they sat locked in a one-room house, waiting to be auctioned. Some produced a plan to run away on the next hawing moon! This would give the running slaves the advantage because on that night, every animal would be singing at the moon, so no one would notice the sounds of tree branches moving to help the slaves reach their destination. The next night, they did that!

Time to Leave

When night came, the moon seemed as bright as ever! This night was an ordinary night, only as if God Himself was prepared to help us on this special night. Now the night's moon was at its highest peak, shining through the quarter's window, and everyone (people of power) assumed to be asleep! We now knew it was time to start our journey for freedom! Once one of the yard workers opened the door of the quarters, some of the plantation workers spoke up to say that some of us wanted to stay and found ourselves a delightful home and people to work for, like Mr. Heath! Little did they know, the Heath family was no more but only the past. So only a few started on the journey for freedom. Uncle June, a hardworking man that plowed the fields for years, saw most of this family die on this plantation. Kids passed away while working in the fields, and the wife gave birth to her last child! Ms. Louse was a midwife and a medicine lady on the plantation. I was so tired of making the best medicine to be sold to the ungrateful townspeople. Mr. and Mrs. Johnson wanted their two kids to grow up and not see Mommy and Daddy crying at night for being abused in front of the locals when coming to the plantation.

Finally, the newest couple, the Ushers, wanted to start a family in a place where they can live where the family could sleep in separate rooms and not worry about who might break the door down in the middle of the night to take their women. They all set off through the night while running for hours now, seeing the sun coming up, drained from dehydration, and sore from moving about the sharp and angled brushes that crossed their path to freedom. The only food that they had, they gave to the kids to keep them from crying so it would not alarm the slave retrievers. As they began to see the mountain in view, they also came up to what looked like small a cottage in the darkest deep part of the woods. Now they were getting closer, not knowing who may come to charge them. The slaves grew tired and weak, losing all sense of direction. They just had to rest somewhere that was not out in the open, where they could be seen by the bounty hunters. While the mountain was in view, the slaves somehow knew that freedom was close by, not hearing the barking of day. They were longing for a time to rest. Mr. June was looking into the window of an incredibly old cottage, with moss covering the windows!

Out came a small-framed, malnourished, old, white woman, with layers of clothes that smelled as if the chimney smoke in powerful vinegar to keep the dogs away. This lady came to the door, looking them up and down while she saw the hurt and the need for food in their weary eyes. She looked over her right shoulder and saw that Mr. June was not alone. A sense of wanting to help came over her. She saw a tear started rolling down the cheek of one woman's face, remembering her (the old, white lady) passed to sure their safety with her she said, "I mean you no harm. We are all both equal children in this troubled time!"

The oldest gentleman, Mr. June, was standing in front of the small lady with such grace and spoke to her in such a manner that he said, "Madame, would you allow us to pass and not alert anyone of our whereabouts? We will appreciate it."

The old lady nodded with a smile and spoke, "I will do better than that!" She also said that she would help them to reach their destination, "So to the mountain where you will all travel. No man may have ever survived the weather as long as the animals that lurk in the wild are looking for food." She told them, once they crossed the river at the base of the mountain, never to look back because the river would never look the same again. "Also, do not look back because your life will never be the same." That is when she handed the youngest boy a stone and said, "Here, take this stone! Once everyone has made it safely over the other side of the river, then place the stone in the last person's footprint! This would secure you all freedom, not worrying about anyone trying to take you and your family back to this angry world."

That night, they rested for the journey in the cottage with the old lady. The runaways fell into a deep sleep and dreamed like no other. When they awoke the next morning, the old lady was nowhere to be found. Early that morning, the slaves started once again at an energic pace of gathering their belongings. While they were traveling down a long narrow foggy path and the wind blowing softly, it seemed like they heard a whisper in their ear, saying, "I'm granting you all safe passage on your safe journey, as my life is ready to take my final rest! I was chosen to prolong my life to save your family, which will be my final token to pass over the Jordon River. Now, to say I give you all the power to survive the living conditions of the northern mountains, I give you the strait of the deadliest bear that comes out of hibernation. Your body will be able to adapt to the weather changes as well. And hide from the most dangerous mountain lion. With this body armor, your family will be able to travel in the thickest part of the woods and not even get the smallest of cuts on your skin. Your eyesight will have the best night vision and be able to see from afar at your most dangerous enemy. Your nose can sniff out the deepest mole that catches a meal underground." The old lady also went on and said that "you would continue with these gifts for as long as you will let no one cross the river into your world."

The Old Lady of the Woods

The lady of the woods wasn't always a scary witch! She was once known to be the future doctor of Chaney Town's medicine lady. This young lady, Gwendolen, started a very privileged upbringing. Her family was well-known in the community. They were part owners of the most well-known stagecoach business. Not wanting to go into the family business, she decided to become a doctor to help the locals of the town. Staring her career off, she was so determined that her male peers weren't going to get in her way! So she studied more and worked harder, even on her breaks from her books and chores. Young lady Gwendolen always loved hiding in a small corner of the woods, where no one could bother her and read cases (good and bad) of surges. A few years passed, and Gwendolen started training beside the best doctors that come far and near to participate in unexplained cases of illness and study the illness cases of the slaves they purchased from the incoming slave ships. Young Gwen started loving everything that has to do with exploring the human body, until one day…

Not all senior male doctors were pleased with women as doctors. But since young Gwen was the daughter of the town's head doctor, everyone just kept their opinion about the lady doctor to themselves. But this one senior doctor who came from out of town didn't feel that he should be quiet about the new changes that were taking place in this town of a female doctor. Now Mr. Adam (traveling physician) knew that if women were now becoming doctors in this small town, it would soon become a wide-controlling way of life that says, if women's voices become greater, then they would eventually set the slave free or give them the right to read and evenly become opinionated. This must not happen on this watch! That was when he came up with a plan for young Gwen to stand in the next human experiment that would be held the next night at an old farmer's barn miles off a dirt road.

This private meeting place took place at different locations so that the locals wouldn't become aware of what took place and who was behind all the experiments. Once the doctors, along with the surgeons, found locations to meet secretly, then they would ask some of the slave owners to sell the slaves that they might have had problems trying to run away or the ones that the plantation owner did not have any use for (too old). The doctors would round them up and take them to the designated place where they would perform surgeries and test new drugs on them. Depending on the doctor that would experiment that night, they would decide if the subject they were performing on needed pain medication or be placed under the substance of anesthesia. The older doctors that had performed at many of these secret outings would always request for the runaway slaves so that they would work on them with no medication in satiation or hurt them in the worst way. That night, the doctor performed three surgeries in which two slaves died on the table while asking them to spare their life. Young lady Gwen had seen all that she could see in her entire lifetime. This made this young girl wonder how a human could become so without remorse for another human being. At that moment, what the young lady had seen made her rethink her future path in such a way. Her decision would not be for only one race's greater good! That night, she set out not only to study one kind of medicine for humanity but medicine from across the world. With her heart still filled with the pain of what she saw that night in the barn, she now started to practice dark magic medicine. This test of time was a huge turning point in her young life. As years passed, the townspeople could never understand why most of the local doctors that were there that night, performing the horrible surgeries and experiments on those helpless slaves, were mysteriously finding themselves jumping off the town's bridge. Young Gwen's life hadn't been the same since! Getting deeper into her dark practice, her young life began to change for the worse in her outer as well as her inner soul.

Coming up to the next part of their journey, Mr. June noticed how the temperature started to change in the middle of the year's hottest season. The wood started to look as if it was a mesomorph with no life. As we could hear from afar running water, Betty (the wife of the youngest married couple), noticed at this point that we had been traveling for about two days now, and no one mentioned that they were tired or hungry! While noticing the air smelled unusually sweet, they heard the river getting louder as they came closer to the river.

Now, the moment arrived of the amazing river that was told in this old lady's story, a magical river that had great power and great beauty, butt everyone's eyes didn't see just that! What they saw at the river was a wild, angry river that was in so much rag that it was like a dam breaking up the steam. Now everyone was thinking that the lady was sending them on a fairy-tale run. But in the need to keep traveling, they started gathering all their belongings by tying their belongings for safety to cross the violent river.

The Other Side

The first one to cross was the young man with the rock. Once his feet touched the cold, crisp water. With great surprise, the river calmed down and welcomed him with peace, giving everyone a sign of stillness and safe crossing. Once everyone was across, the young man remembered what the lady said to do with the rock! He then placed the rock on the last footprint of the last person that stepped out of the water on part of the land that was foretold in the old lady's story of a world that no one had ever known existed! Everyone's eyes were as wide as a cork on a wine syrup jar, and their mouths were taking in the mushy cold air, as if they were locked in a large ice chest, mesmerized in being at the foot of a mountain that they had never seen in their life! Glancing back at the river that they just crossed, they couldn't believe their eyes. Once more, the river that they had just crossed was so breathtaking! The bold colors came out of the water, which they had never witnessed before! The beautiful lines of fish were as if a parade of colors dancing down the stream, while the water was giving off a soft sound of harmony. The tree on this site was rich green and wasn't faced by the snow and the coldness of the wind that greeted us when we first arrived. Everything that surrounded us was in the high energy of great beauty. Not knowing where to go, suddenly there came a glow, something that seemed like fireflies coming down off a hill, landing in a line, leading up to this opening of a door of what looked like a cave! Not becoming scared at this point, we begin to walk alongside the fireflies to see where they would take us so we can hurry to get out of the cold. Now, coming up to a cave opening that wasn't seen in plain sight gave us chills of not knowing what might come running out to attack us and having nothing to defend against the danger.

The Transformation

Now we were standing at the doorway of this breathtaking cave that had such structure, as if someone had carved the entrance by hand (beautiful)! It was nothing that our eyes had ever laid upon. To describe the things that we saw in front of us, we couldn't start comparing them with anything we'd ever seen. The walls were spotted with glass-like jewelry that gave off colors in place for light all around us in such a manner that we knew where to place our feet as we walked inside, seeing the life of greenery growing around, as if we were standing in the middle of August field. To hear fresh water falling from the top of an opening, as if it was helping to sustain life within itself. We began to walk over to take a sip of water while noticing life living all around in this pond. There were fish of all colors and plants that were growing in this pond that gave off pulsating light, as if they were helping something to stay alive through them! The air was filled with freshness, the smell of flowers, and a sweet hint of honey. At this moment, we all realized that we were meant to arrive here on this day with the eight slaves happy and accepting this place called home. Everyone fell to their knees, giving God thanks for saving us and giving them such a great gift of a new life! That's when things started to change for them. First, it was elder June passing out into a deep sleep; next, Ms. Nadia, the elder lady of medicine! No one was able to wake them from their deep sleep! Suddenly, their bodies started taking the form of something that seemed not human! This shook everyone else up to where they started to run out of the cave, but they didn't make it too far! That's when a force grabbed hold of them, and they started to feel their bodies take form. Their skin started to stretch and fill up with great strength and twitching; their skin were printed with gold dye. They could also feel their hair transforming straight and long, as if someone or something was giving them this power of how things needed to be done!

Once all the transformations had taken place, everybody there was lying on the floor of the mountain cave, awakened to wonder if it was safe to get up! When everyone started to sit up and catch their breath, they realized that nothing would be the same anymore. When they realized that they were okay, the next thing they thought about was Mr. June and Ms. Nadia! The younger people got up and rushed over to where they saw them but only found two very large dogs lying still but only breathing slowly. They first began to think that the two large dogs might have eaten the two elders, but nothing appeared to be as it seems in this cave. That's when the two (Mr. June and Ms. Nadia) awoke and started to lift themselves, only to realize that they were not themselves anymore!

Mr. June said, "Not trying to give me a heart attack, but what am I?"

Even though his mouth was not moving, we could understand him! Now what was going on with us and this cave one of the youngest applied. When the large dogs stood on their feet, that's when they realized they weren't dogs at all! They were werewolves! With such beauty, their coats were so thick and flowing, and their marking was so detailed to where you would only hear out of storybooks of stories of powerful kings and queens! As we watched them stand, all our hearts were telling us to bow. We did just that! And when we bowed, our bodies began to put on a light show, as if we were honored by the most high himself!

Now testing our newfound abilities, all the males' bodies in our families were so broad that it looked like they were wearing a suit of armor under their skin! The markings on their bodies were so detailed that it shined gold when they get angry! When it was time to hunt, they would transform into hunting wolves with the same detailed marking on their skin, which would now become fur! With the inability to talk, the transformed warrior (known as soldiers) translated to each other with their minds, which made it easier in the group and did not bring attention to their prey. The soldiers' job was to keep predators away from coming too close to their living area, which might cause harm to our people while hunting and fishing.

They must remember the only rule they had when hunting, it was only to kill elderly animals, because they had lived a full life and produced enough offspring to carry on for the next generations. All these rules came about to the newfound freedom to give this beautiful place time to rejuvenate itself, as well as there was no blessing in chains from caging animals and taking away the lifestyle here on earth. Meanwhile, women were all treated as queens as they would take care of the gardens and the everyday lifestyle of the new land as they teach their young, most and foremost was honoring the elders daily. This was the most important of all because if it wasn't for them the decision they made, and the action they had to endure of bringing us to this point! We honor them for reaching us to this newfound freedom was the best and because of this! Every night, after a good meal, they sang and danced about their past cultural life, giving praise to the Highest (God)!

Life in the new land was great for a few years until everyone noticed the same number of people that arrived here! No one was able to bring forth a new generation (kids). The elderly were all well over their seasons in baring kids, and the youngest ones were brothers and sisters. They were all together cousins. This made it very difficult to bring forth a new generation to enjoy the cultural experience of life here on this mountain with the blessing of no one was able to die but only able to grow old and turn into a wolf. They all continued to give thanks for what god had blessed them with and carry on seeing what the years would bring! This made the young kids very sad about not knowing they would ever have a mate for themselves. That's when a glow appeared on the cave wall, as if the mountain was speaking to them. When one of the elders approached for a closer view of the glow, that's when he noticed it was lettering that was carved in the wall in their form of speech that they understood! It said, "To grow in numbers, one will have to mate with an outsider upon the mountain's approval!" You will know the approval as everything would receive a blessing of strength, and more things would grow in great numbers. This pleased everyone with great joy! With that said, how would someone know to look for this mountain or even know which direction to travel to find this place? Looking back at our situation, if the mountain brought us here, it can choose someone to travel the same path as we did.

Students

Sharon: A scientology major, a true-to-her-study geek, a very detailed person of science. Her classmates felt that she needed to take a break from her studies and live a little outside the box.

Trudy: A psychology major, a very beautiful young lady working on the last semester of her doctoring degree! She was a very soft-spoken young lady with a gift for making people lower their stress levels with the tone of her voice and the beauty of her eyes!

Rickey: A teacher of agricultural business. He was always on the search for crossbreeding and breakthroughs of finding plants and species of life to heal the very ill and make life better for people living in the new-age (2000s) way of life.

During a lecture in class one semester, these students heard of such a place by a professor that was foretold hidden in a mountain that had such healing powers. That mountain (that was named the Maypop Mountain) was like a paradise to many, a place where you would never die. Some people say that they had seen wolves that were so much larger than the average-size wolf. You would never see them as they could see you coming over fifty or more yards away. But the professor again told the student to be warned! No man has ever placed their foot on his ground because of the great magic force surrounding the area. This gave Sharon more determination to go and view this paradise.

The Maypop Mountain got its name from an old, small-framed man named Adam Williams that lived at the bottom of the mountain. This man lived with his wife, along with the scene of the river and the mountain in the backdrop of his home! They have been living there for several years since their children all grew up and had moved away from home and were raising their own family now! Mr. Adam and this family were placed on this land for a special reason. This reason came about because of the wise tale of the Maypop Mountain magic it holds. Many people started hearing of this place during this age when money was very hard to come by! Even farmers had a hard time growing and selling their crops. During the mid-1800s, when there was a great drought and the need to buy seeds to farm the lands, people were searching for any breakthrough (magic, hidden treasure, or even a new development that no one's ever heard of) that they could come across and change their lives forever. So when many people heard of this mountain, people from across the globe came in search of treasure! Travelers started in search of this place but had never heard of it since, which made this small village start to look bad, of all the travelers coming through this town and to never be seen again! The townspeople came together and elected a person to lure the travelers to the opposite direction of Maypop Mountain. So they all agreed to give Mr. Adam twenty acres of land for him and his family, twelve castles, and twenty-four chickens in honoring them like royalty for saving this town's good name. To seal the deal, they (the townspeople) placed their signature Maypop flower on the left side of their chests and gave his right hand a firm handshake with a great smile of thanks for doing this for them.

Why this flower? Well, this flower was different from the average flowers you may have seen in your garden. This flower was a breath of life that some say represents scriptures of the Holy Bible! As it once said in Matthew 14:13–21 how Jesus fed five thousand of his followers with only three fish and five loaves of bread. That's why they chose this flower cause of the flower itself, through beauty and living proof of truth behind his words. The description of the flower has three stigmas on top coming from the style. (This represents the Bible's three fish.) Below the stigma, there were five filaments (this represents the five loaves of bread in the Bible) now moving down the flower to where the beautiful overlays of color were, where you would find streams of peddles growing out in all directions of the plant! This represents the five thousand people (of all colors) feeding on Jesus's gift. That is why the mountain was named after this flower, in honor of the gift of life it can provide.

The Permission

Curiosity had overtaken Sharon's mind since the lecture in class. She came up with this idea with her two best friends (Ricky and Trudy) to travel a study for the university to bring forth somewhat the truth about this place that was blessed by God himself! Now placing their minds together to come up with a study project so eye-catching, the university board couldn't resist saying no! The three best friends began to write up a proposal to promise to bring back all the findings and place them under the university name. They would be looking for new plants that no one had ever seen or heard of! Findings, such as bowls, tools, or even animals that no one had ever seen. The reason to explore this place was that it was said to have healing powers and jewels and to bring the finds and the bragging rights back to this university, as well as introduce new medicine to this generation. The committee was somehow very interested in the findings that may exist. So the university committee approved the travel study in helping the school create dictation, to bring back photos, objects of such proof that there was such a place with unbelievable powers.

Ricky, Sharon, and Trudy started packing immediately, even though they were set to leave the following week. During this time, they gathered up clothes that would sustain them through all different types of weather. The foods they packed were unperishable types of foods, along meds and first aid kits. They also thought of bringing things to trade with the town's locals for trade and to build the trust of the townspeople. Reaching local townspeople through books of history and the Internet, they found a lot of information on the way of life, in fishing, and trading in the nearby towns.

The Village Peoples

One of the professors of the school there overheard the students' travel! He had heard of this place before when he was just a student himself. Mr. Hardeman (the professor) wanted to speak with the group that was leaving in search of this powerful place to make them aware of their voyage! He began to tell them about a teacher from a college that he attended years back who set out on the search of this same place on this same mountain that was once said to be unreachable by men! The teacher also set out with a group of friends and was never heard from again! A search party was set out to retrieve answers to the whereabouts of the traveling party. All they were able to do was spend too much time and money with the locals and leave with no answers. The thing about local people is that they didn't care about new people arriving in their town and trying to change their way of life.

This village was a small city that had a population of one thousand people. No one owned cars. They made runs to a nearby town for trading in horses and buggies. The locals always believed that keeping the tradition of their way of life would be keep the low number of sickness in the little town. People that lived there were mostly farmers of a rich ground of land that never dries. Local village people were small in stature. They taught themselves different languages and laws to protect their town from outsiders that brought legal action to them, trying to purchase their land without their knowledge. Therefore, they thought newcomers arriving in their town brought bad luck to them. In search of the legend of the Maypop Mountain, some locals have said that they from time, think that they have spotted living life on the mountain, but always no proof or evidence of life living on the mountain. They also believed that if enough travelers would come in search of this mythical place, this would disturb their homes and way of life (bringing bad luck to their land and animals). When travelers came for direction, they always directed them to the forbidden mountain, knowing that once they leave to start their journey, they wouldn't ever return to be able to tell more of their colleagues about this place.

Arriving at the First Village

Once Sharon, Trudy, and Ricky reached a long tiring voyage on the plane, the airline workers told them that they would have to take a truck taxi to arrive at a small city called Nelson City. This drive would be an hour drive to reach this place. Traveling on a once paved road, which was now a driving road, with bumps and dust flinging from the taxi tires as it moved at such speed. Not able to sleep or rest, the students set their excitement on their upcoming adventure. Arriving two hours later, tired and dirty, the young students didn't hesitate to walk up to an elderly local named Ms. Minnie (a local tailor), asking for directions to Maypop Mountain, not wanting to talk to Sharon because of the watchful eyes of the locals watching her! But Ms. Minnie was one of the townspeople had a soft heart from a young age that was curious about learning the history of new lands. She (Ms. Minnie) began to talk about the towns and their people to avoid the conversation on the mountain until Rickey interrupted and asked about Maypop Mountain. Silence came over to the surrounding townsmen that overheard the conversation that they were having. With that said, Ms. Minnie ended the history lesson and began to walk off, as if they weren't standing there. The students then realized that every local was staring at them, as if they had done something wrong. At that moment, the students immediately grabbed their belongings to gain time to arrive in the next town before it got too late.

Late noon, they just arrived at another town called Chaney town! This town was no bigger than the last owner that we just ventured from. But in this town, the people made a living out of fishing. As we came closer to town, people stared at us as to be expected! Everyone ran up to us, trying to sell us everything that they had to offer, until Trudy was suddenly guided into a hut by a little boy with only a few words that she could understand.

"Come! Come! Grandpa talk," he said, noticing a young boy was guiding Trudy into a hut. The others placed things that they were planning to but went back to follow her to the hut for everyone's safety. Once they entered the hut, they were introduced to all kinds of herbs and liquids in bottles as candles flicked across the room. Now everyone was in the hut. They noticed, sitting in the center of the room was a well-aged man with his eyes closed but was well awake! The student stood in the hut while admiring their surroundings, not knowing what to say to the old man. So he (wise man) started to speak to them, saying, "I know why you are here! You are seeking the riches of Maypop Mountain."

He began to tell them that through the years, travelers had searched for the same thing. They set out, traveling the same way, but had never been heard of since. He also told them that their journey would be different! They carried with them what the other voyagers did not have. The wise man went on to tell them about how the Maypop Mountain must accept you for you to enter. The powers that surrounded this mountain were created from the cries of the early slaves. It was said that he came down and placed his hand on the top of the mountain and gave it incredible powers. But the only way anyone could enter is by the cry of one predator that felt remorse for the prey, who should grant a safe passage entering this beautiful place! As he faced over in Trudy's direction, he told her that her beauty would become of great use to want ever holds on the other side. Then he looked at Sharon and said, "Once you make it back, you will succeed in what you are searching for, but the fame will be so great that you ask yourself if it is worth letting the powerful people know about your discovery."

Now directing the words over to young Ricky, he began to tell him that his steps might be cut short, and he might not see the other side, but he told him this: Stay by the river. And in three days, he would play the most important role that would take him down in the history books with great rewards. As they turned to leave the hut, they felt that now they were headed on the right path.

Entering the Woods

After a long dusty ride, on the back of one local farmer's truck, they now had come to the beginning of their forest destination. While collecting their gear, they couldn't help but know how the wind had picked up. And the trees were swaying side by side, as if they were welcoming them. The forest that they must travel to was one with the most secrets that had not yet been revealed, starting on their journey in the woods while ignoring the "beware" signs, thinking like some teen, as if everything was for laugh! They began to make humor out of every sign they came by: *(1) Beware, the forest plays many games with you, and you will never win! (2) Beware of the old witch's spirit! She never likes the ones that carry their souls around! (3) Enter this forest! You will never get hungry, but the wild animals will!* Paying no attention to the signs, Sharon and her crew started to follow a narrow path where their faith would guide them safely through their journey!

Walking for five hours now, the team decided to rest in a beautiful area of the woods, covering the ground like a quilted blanket, covering the grounds with colors. The weather was so nice; it winded as if royalty was entering the room on the red carpet for the first time.

After the hour of rest, they started to continue once again to travel deeper into the wood to make up for the time they lost during the early break before the sun went down. Later that evening, Sharon, Trudy, and Rickey all agreed that it was getting too late for traveling in the woods. Trudy happened to look down and saw an old broken piece of wood with something written on it! The writing was another warning sign: Beware! You have reached the home of the old Chaney Town's witch doctor! That's when they noticed lies ahead, about thirty feet away, an old abandoned cottage just behind some bushes or shrubbery. While taking great interest in the old place, they weren't aware that this was the home of a real old witch lady! Being young and not thinking of any dangers, Trudy walked over to hold in the home structure that would give her the ability to view the inside of the cottage, hoping to find value inside that would be interesting to place in the museum back home. All that Trudy saw were pots of all sizes on the table and floor, and she was able to see bottles of many subjects, as if they were waiting to be used in spearmint. The fireplace seemed like it hadn't seen much action in many years. That's when Ricky realized a unique glow that was coming around the back of the old cabin.

Once around the backyard of the cottage, Ricky saw several beautiful glass bottles of many colors hanging from a tree, moving from side to side as the wind blew quietly. He didn't think anything of it, just that someone who used to live here was trying to scare off some animals. They did not know the real reason for the colored bottles that were created for them several years ago to place them on the right path in fulfilling the prediction of the old witch. While still behind the cottage, admiring the bottles, the team began to realize that a small amount of fog was around their feet. It appeared out of nowhere but was coming from the opposite direction of what the townspeople told them to go. Ricky started to walk, his feet down the path of the fog, only to be stopped by Sharon, feeling the need to make came for tonight. Everyone agreed and started to bulk down (getting out their sleeping bags) for the night. They all had different moments of curiosity about where the path would lead them.

Now that they had settled into place for the night, and the team just finished with dinner, they made it under the light of the moon while resting around the campfire. Trudy was busy studying the collection that she gathered from the old cabin: First was a four-foot-long stick that was well encrypted with drawings and writings on it! Second was an old book that was sitting alone on a stand with an odd type of leather that was holding the pages together. Once opened, in it were different types of what looked like good spells, and some were dark spells! Trudy started to read some of the spells that she could recognize. One that captured her eye was making a large area deceived (make disappear) by the human eyes. The last was necklace. It was well designed and had glass all under the bottom structure of it. It would be very interesting for the museum exhibit. As her eyes got heavy, feeling sleepy, young Trudy decided to place everything back in the bag. But she wanted to wear the necklace around her neck. As they snuggled into their sleeping bags, Ricky agreed to be the first lookout as the others slept for the first part of the night. Trudy began to fall into a deep sleep and started to dream of a place that she had never visited before. This place was so beautiful that the trees and animals were all glowing with a soft glazing glow. As she walked toward the lake, Trudy looked suddenly over her shoulder as she felt that someone or something might have been watching her. Now standing at the lake, she noticed that this was no average lake that was shining up at her. The rays from the sun and the slow waves from the water slowly danced together hand in hand. This force of nature that her eyes had seen was nothing but beauty. Young Trudy started to reach into the lake to see if everything that was going on was real! Behold! To her surprise, she saw an image behind her, a figure of a wild animal. Now as she made a quick turn, no one was there! While she was still in a deep sleep, she was making movements, as if she was having a bad dream. That's when Ricky noticed that the necklace that Trudy had on was coming to life! The necklace was lit up, as if it was waiting on her for a lifetime. Ricky then rushed over to Trudy to wake her up to see what was going on with the necklace that she was wearing. When Trudy's eyes were clear to see what was happening around her neck, she immediately threw the necklace away from her in fear of something that could happen to her! Then she realized she couldn't leave the necklace behind, so she then placed it in her bag for safekeeping. As the night ended, several eyes awakened with anticipation of starting the journey down the mysterious path. With sleepiness still in their eyes for several attempts to take quick naps due to all the excitement of wondering what this path would hold. They all were filled with anticipation to get packed and loaded to start on this interesting path.

Now packed and ready to travel, Trudy, with her camera, did not want to leave anything to the naked eye! As they started entering this foggy path, they noticed how the weather suddenly changed. Miles down the path, the fog became clearer. The trees began to look more like albinos (pale in color), and the bushes were looking as if the weather surprised them with a cold winter. That didn't stop anyone from deciding to turn back from exploring this great adventure. Later that evening, after traveling over twelve miles into the forest, we became aware of the sound of water rushing downstream. Another sound that grabbed their attention was the echoing around them, not knowing what direction it was coming from. Trying not to get too distracted by the sounds that the forest was making, to stay on course, they had to get out our technical instruments to keep their directions and location of their whereabouts in the woods. Knowing about some of the dangers, they were well prepared and ready to face them head-on. After a long hard day of cutting back bushes and stepping over falling trees, they finally reached the river that they heard miles away.

The River

This river didn't seem to look like anything out of the ordinary! Catching an image in the water, Sharon leaned closer to better understand what swimming was. Even though the river was a rapid current, the fish that was swimming by seemed to have been swimming as if they were in a small pond. Not thinking of anything suspicious, she continued prepping her belongings to secure them before they crossed the river. While Ricky placed air into the raffle on their voyage to cross the river, Sharon and Trudy discussed how and why it was important to cross at the lowest part of the river where the current was at the lowest. After placing their ideas together, they thought that throwing a rope across the river was best to protect them from being washed downstream by the current. Everyone agreed on this method as they gathered in a circle, holding hands for a quick word of prayer for their safe passage to cross the river. (Little did they know, by doing this, a word of prayer permitted them to enter the other side of the mountain safely.) This made the river a little calm, and the wind stopped!

Now the boat was ready to float, and the rope was secured in place across the river. The three students (Sharon, Trudy, and Ricky) were all placed, not knowing that all was gripping their ore so tight in fear of not knowing what dangers the river would put them in. There was one talking, for the focus was all about staying in the boat and riding the current (keeping the boat steady) at the right time while not crashing onto the rocks. Everything didn't seem strange for the first mile down to where Trudy got her camera out to take pictures of the beautiful surroundings. While Ricky and Sharon were in a heated debate, Trudy thought she had seen something or someone watching them from the outside of the river. But when she zoomed her camera in for a closer look, nothing was there. That's when they all noticed the water was picking up speed as they prepared themselves for a rough terrace downstream. Now we were traveling at a rapid speed! Noticing the swirls of the undertow in great quantity made them not want to fall out of their boat anytime now for fear of getting pulled under by the undertow and drowning. Dealing with fighting the rapids for over twenty minutes now, everyone grew tired with not enough strength to hold the ore in the water to guide them away from the rocks. The raffle started taking on water as the students began to be tossed around with no energy to fight the current. Suddenly, the raffle hit against a rock, tossing everyone out in different directions. Trying to stay afloat, while calling out everybody's names, the water allowed Sharon to come up for a breath of air. That was when she saw Rickey holding on to a rock, trying to lift himself to safety, reaching out his hand, as if he was trying to grab ahold of her hand while she continued to travel downstream. Sharon, now getting exhausted and still trying to fight with the water, captured a glimpse of Trudy a couple of yards away, waving her hand at her, calling for help. That's when she went down under the water for the last time, being pulled under by an undertow. This current was so great that all her hard work fighting to stay afloat was like she wasn't fighting at all. Not remembering anything else, her last thought was a chance for her friend to make it alive to tell her family the story of how she died.

On Strange Land

Not aware of the land that she (Sharon) just arrived at, there she lay on the edge of a lake, not knowing whether she was alive or dead. But after a minute or two, she began to coughed up some water that she had drunk while riding alone with the undertow. With the fresh air that she started taking into her lungs, her eyes began to create the strength to open! Sharon's focus wasn't clear, but she noticed that she had arrived on a beach with sand that wasn't the kind of sand back home. The amazing sand was like small rocks and had a pearlized gloss on them. She held her head up for a better view when she knew that she wasn't on an average beach. The trees were all healthy and had illuminated lighting on them. That minute, Sharon thought that she was in heaven! That's when she started calling her friends' names, hoping that they were close by, not noticing her leg was bleeding due to the injury she sustained underwater while fighting to survive. But no one answered her calls. That's when she saw someone coming out of the wood, walking toward her, as if she was an injured seal lying on the beach. The gentleman was walking up to her with a startled look on his face, as if he had not seen her before. This person walking toward her was dark in skin tone, tall, with a wide upper body, and his complete body structure was like a gladiator straight off a movie screen. That's when Sharon asked to go to a hospital so she could get medical care right before she fainted with exhaustion.

When she awakened this time, she was not lying on the beach but on a bed of large leaves, with her leg wrapped where her cut was. Not knowing how she got there and humbling, she was sitting beside her! Sharon then looked over at him as she lay on the ground to ask him, "What place is this?" But he didn't answer, not familiar with the language she was speaking. He didn't seem happy to see me but looked like he wanted to kill me after he got the information he needed out of her! As she was looking around to find something she could use as a weapon in case she might need it, she began to tell him who she was, a student from a college in search of the truth about a mountain called Maypop Mountain. He replied, "Why look for this such place?" speaking to her in broken English, back in the same time zone when they first came to this land, not knowing that she came from the time six generations ahead of him. He then reached over and placed moss on her open wound to protect her cut. While he gave her some water to drink, he only thought of him helping her get better to kill her all over again. After drinking the water, Sharon suddenly felt like her body was healing itself from the inside out! Thinking that he might have poisoned her, she then got up and was positioned to run. But when the moss fell off her leg, she noticed that her wound was healed. That is when she asked him what this place was called. He replied, "This is such a place that is blessed by God himself." He also continues to say that "his family was the only ones that have been living here alone for many years now. "How did you find this place?"

"Our family was chosen to enter here, the door of this mountain."

Then he replied, "How did you enter?"

Sharon was unable to answer him. She didn't know how she arrived, but all she could answer was by saying that she was being carried by an undertow in the river. After that, he introduced himself. "Greetings. My name is Jordon. I am one of the elder sons from our manor." He began to tell her that he was one of the two soldiers they had here at this place of living, that his family always told the young generation that once an outsider arrived on this mountain, that's would change their ways of living to extinction. That's when Sharon noticed his cloth was thick, dried-out terry type of clothing with no color to them. But his body frame was telling her that he worked out daily. The incredible markings on his body were so amazing. The ink that the artist used was black, dipped in gold flakes. Sharon noticed that when he changed his emotion, it seemed that his markings wanted to stand up for war. (The pattern would change.) All the details were interesting. Through all these findings, she couldn't help but wonder if her friends were safe.

Meanwhile, Trudy's body had washed up miles away on the same beach. With the help of the local fish, they pushed her body under what looked like an old beaver cave so that the local land animals wouldn't mistake her for dinner. There, Trudy could regain her strength and service this new land. With the air knocked out of her lungs, Trudy was only weak and dazed from the currents that brought her to this place where she slept for days before she would be found. The surround of the beaver cave was so unique and complex. The beaver cave was arranged so that on a sunny day, the cave would give off cool, soft light to keep the beavers cool so they wouldn't become hot. And for the chilly nights, the cave itself knew just when to change colors to warm whoever might occupy the beaver cave at that moment.

Now Rickey was left back at the river, holding on to a rock with a death grip, and then somehow managed to grab a hold of the rope that they had to pull to the other side. With tiredness setting upon him, Rickey then swam to the side where they started their water adventure. He couldn't help crying, thinking that he was the only survivor. As he came down, he gathered his thoughts on how he was going back to tell everyone that his colleagues didn't make it. He hated the fact that he would have to be the one to tell how they died. So he decided to stay by the riverbank to collect his thoughts before he got the courage to go back by himself. Later, by the fire Rickey made for himself, he began to remember what the old man in the village told him to do. He remembered staying behind for three days at the river. If this moment was for told to him! While it might've not been for him to enter the mountain, help them leave it. So he did just that, waiting for the next three days by the side of the riverbank.

The Manor

The manor was their village, where all the founding family south out refuge when they first arrive at Maypop Mountain. Through many generations that they all lived through, their immortal lives had come across new-age animals in and out of the waters. Some strange things had arrived by the current of the waters. Finding out what they were used to and why gave them great joy and something to wonder about how life was going on the outer side. But no one's ever thought or even spoken about traveling back to today's land because they would be meeting up with death! Their only mortality was as long as they stayed within the mountain. The water that arrived at the pond inside the mountain would heal any ailment that any person might have, such as a cut or sickness upon the body. If any outsider stumbled upon this pond, then the healing powers would bring war to their community. The flowers they had here surrounding their mountain would cleanse the body overnight. And rubbing the flowers, especially the maypop, repeddled your skin, would produce its healthiest form and change the body's pigmentation. Even the stones that held this cave together placed a big part of riches for the outside human. The stones had minerals, and jewelry could be made from them for a very large price. When placed over a cut, the moss would heal the cut in a matter of minutes. The animal would not attack, for they saw no harm from their tribe. The air all year round was sweet in smell.

Even though it was cold outside the mountain, they had not ever shivered. The elders said that if you climb to the peak of this mountain in the morning while the sun was rising, you would get the chance to view life on the other side of the river. But the gift that the mountain gave them was that the other side couldn't see them. Once they had a feast on their day of rest, they would not hunger for the next five days. These days would come for the animals to populate and had no reason for extinction. This enabled them to not live by bread alone when it came to survival here. That is why, when the tribal elders reached a certain age, they would permanently transform into wolves. This was considered the highest level (rank) that God could offer them. They would become blessed with the great ability of prophecy, the strength that had no limits, speed like no other animal could ever have, and even shapeshifters when they needed to. While others saw the elders as those with great honor, they shouldn't work hard to keep others safe. That's why they came up with the younger men as soldiers. The young women were creators; they made things for when the starting of fertility they would have plenty of room and platforms for growth to educate our new blessings, kept them with plenty of work while also keeping a watchful eye out for the wild wolves that wanted to enter the cave to become mortal.

These wild wolves were the only problem that the tribe had when it came to their paradise on Maypop Mountain. These wild beasts believed that if they get the stone neckless from the old witch of the mountain and combined the maypop signature flower while standing in the pond of life that sat in the center of the cave, the colony would have the same ability as the tribe of the cave. Every generation that came made the wild wolves grow more and more aggressive to start a war with the mountain colony. This wolf pack was led by a leader named Darius. That was the only one that cared to become immortal. The other wolf didn't see any sense of this, but they were only engaged of entering paradise for the buffet of food over there. These wolves that were led by Darius were known as the nation wolves. The leader, Darius, went out to retrieve as many far-off areas to recruit as many different wolves as possible with different war tactics to combine to go back to his land to defeat the Maypop Mountain tribe.

Now he was back with more wolf soldiers, ready to take over the mountain at Darius's command! As they waited, they underwent intense skills training that they picked up from each colony they had among them. Since the growth of new visiting wolves, Darius knew that he must move in soon to start the war because the food supplies on their mountainside were wearing thin. After months of training, the wolves noticed that their body had become bigger than normal, and their sense had become more intense than when they were back home in their home colony! That gave them an interest in what once they entered the Maypop Mountain, the powers they would have, and the treasure they would come upon! From afar, the wolves sometimes glanced at one of the tribes while hunting on their land. Seeing this for the first time, how they would enter the woods to hunt, and now transform into wolves, their bodies became bigger, and their tribal tattoos became fur when changing to hunt with the great speed. The Trible solder moved through the woods much faster than the average wolves. They noticed their every move and hoped one day they would be able to take over all the luxury they have in that part of the mountain. The leader, Darius, knew of the medicine lady, Nadia, the wisest of them all. He knew, with her by his side, he would ruin that mountain and create a bridge or a portal to be able to leave the side of the mountain and enter. The present townspeople had no idea that they existed, and he would take over the population on the townspeople's land with the idea of moving food and more areas to the population. This would allow Darius to start up a nation where he would be king!

Miss Nadia

Back at the cave, Elder Nadia was creating potions of medicine as a hobby now and trying to create a formula to transform one of the outside wolves into a human to start their population of the new generation to retrieve the extra blessings that God had promised them in making their tribe bigger, as well as the pouring out of great treasures. One day, she (Elder Nadia) was working continuously in her lab (a private corner of the cave) when a soft wind blew past her face. With the ability of prophecy, Miss Nadia was able to read the wind of what it was trying to tell her about what was coming. She picked up that the local wolves were coming together to pose war against them to take over the mountain for the riches it had with it. After years have passed since the crossing of the river to this paradise, Miss Nadia never forgot the hard time living on the plantation. Knowing this, she couldn't let the outsider come to their paradise and bring back slavery all over again. Her heart and power were all for her family's love! This rumor of war would bring the cave to high alert. But before she would bring this to everyone's attention, she must find out the truth and understand with neighboring wolves to retrieve the confirmation on the great wall. Nadia knew that she must meet with Darius herself and get a good understanding of this war and his taking over their home. The thing that they arrive wolves misunderstood about the tribal Queen elder Nadia is that even though she was of age and smaller than her pack, she had been blessed with many gifts in supporting the survival of her tribe. With only the protection of her family in mind, Nadia would give the enemy the chance to resent the war against them. So late one night, Miss Nadia came to Darius in a dream and told him to meet with her alone in the middle of his forest, where the two major rocks were butting heads. She also stated that for his pack's survival, they needed to figure out ways to resolve this so it wouldn't result in losing many of his pack. (In other words, this was not what he wanted.) When Nadia left Darius's dream, this made him mad like never before. If she could come to him in a dream and give him demands, then what else could her powers do to him in this war? That's when she realized, they will meet her face-to-face by the rocks. Once Nadia awakens, she knew that she had to alert everyone about Darius's plans to take over the cave. But first, she went to the wall of life to seek advice on the best way to meet with Darius on the battle issues. But the wall remained silent once again because of knowing that they would make a good choice in winning the war battle of not letting evil into this paradise. Elder Nadia knew that if any of her people got hurt or injured badly, it would be harder to retrieve the blessings to populate their community. As she walked down the hallway to her chamber, she didn't notice how the walls glowed more as she passed by! This was truly a sign that their God was with them and going to continue to be with her. But before she met with Darius that night, she would take with her a bottle of a potion that would make him human for a few hours, hoping this would humble him for not wanting to pursue this war any longer. If this worked, her family would be out of harm's way.

Zax's Discovery

Warrior Zax was a brave warrior from the plantation tribe. His task was to train and keep up with the whereabouts of the neighboring wolves. While sitting camouflaged in the forest, he watched the river wolves fight among themselves over food. As he was sitting silently for hours, his sense began to lead him in another direction to an unfamiliar sound in the beaver territory. Zax was always great with his surrounding animals and their way of life even when they were in harm's way! This wasn't a sound from any animal but a weak (hurt) human. Not knowing if he is running to war or a rescue, Zax instantly transformed into battle mode (forming into a wolf for battle). As he started to run in the direction of the sound, he can help himself by being angry with himself for the thing that one of the native wolves has gotten by him and wreaking havoc on the native animals. At this point, the more racing through his body, the larger he became as his coat (fur) prepared itself for war (glowing brighter with great details), running at top speed to reach the victim in time to save whoever needed help before it was too late! Reaching the point of interest, he noticed that there wasn't anyone around to even growl with but then knew that the weak sound was coming from an old abandoned beaver home on the side of the river. Still thinking an animal was hurt, Zax began to walk up to the old beaver hut, as if someone or something would just go out to battle for the wounded animal. As he came for a closer look, he noted that only an injured young lady lay inside. Zax leaned in for a good look and only found a person that needed to be treated. Her breathing was so shallow, as if the wind was being taken away from her. That's when Zax realized that there wasn't any danger around, and he began to transform back to his human form to render aid to help this person.

With all the fighting to stay on top of the water, Trudy never gave up on life even when she got in trouble and was stuck under the undertow. Now, with all the fighting with the water left her very weak for days now. She slept to get her straight back, not knowing who she might be around or if knowing her life may be in danger. While Trudy lay in the old beaver hut, even though the hut was old but the healing powers of the pieces of sticks and the month it took to build this hut still carry the healing power to keep Trudy's body stable to be found. Once Zax entered the hut through an opening in the water to help render aid if needed to this woman. He turned this young lady on her back to see if that would help to wake her, but that didn't help! He then knew that if he wanted to help save this young lady, he would have to add a little more power to the hut to wake her up. So Zax placed his hand on the edge of the hut and the other hand on the heart of this young woman. Then the most beautiful light brightened the beaver hut while pulsing through his hands and traveling down to this woman's body. In less than a minute, Trudy's eyes again twitched, as if they were finding a way to open. Zax then knew that the extra power that he applied was taking effect, and Trudy's eyes began to open. In a world of seeing a woman that wasn't any kin to him for the first time, Zax's eyes and mouth opened so wide upon seeing the beauty of Trudy's eyes. With the hazel sparkle coming from her eye and her long, thick eyelashes, while darkness surrounded the lining of her eyes, and her eyebrows were perfectly created as you only hear about the life of a queen in the Bible and realize that a real woman from the Bible has arrived on our mountain and is alive and well.

Once Trudy gained back her vision and focus on want was staring back at her, she reacted by crawling to the back of the beaver hut. Her heart raced, not knowing why these strange men were looking to help her or to hurt her! In catching her voice to ask the man what he want, thinking it would send him running way in another direction. Zax just stood there, wondering what tribe she might be from. He then realized he needed to gain her trust; he must look friendly!—not happening! He took his job to control the safety of this mountain and his tribe's security. At that moment, Zax switched into warrior mode and grabbed Trudy by the hand and threw her over his shoulder and headed to take her to the elder to see if and how they were going to destroy this woman, not realizing that this might be the young lady that could help them retrieve the blessing that God promised them. While Zax was traveling in the direction of the cave, on the way to the cave, he couldn't help thinking about how he saw this lady for the first time and how his body started to feel in a way he never felt before. Right then, he stopped and placed her off his shoulder and let her walk to the cave. Trudy, with tears in her eyes, stood up straight and began to walk behind Zax, wondering if her friend was alive or dead and if she was walking her last walk to her death. While walking through the forest, after taking her mind off her friends, Trudy started to pay attention to the beauty and structure of the surrounding forest. It wasn't anything that she had seen before or had read in any of her school textbooks. The animals had no fear of predators, and the plants were very healthy and all living in sequence with each other to better their life. Then she noticed that the temperature was very comfortable, with no chills in the air or heat to make you sweat, as if it was in between seasons. As Trudy walked even closer, noticing the cave in her view, she then looked down at herself to see all the bloodstains on her shirt and pants but did not see any cuts or scars where the blood came from. That's when Trudy started crying all over again, thinking the blood could have been from her friends that could have been hurt somewhere close by, and she was not able to help them. Meanwhile, Zax was walking a few steps ahead of Trudy. Having the ability to read minds, Zax couldn't help but feel what she was going through. That made Zax realize that the tribe wasn't endangered but wanted to get his people to help in the search for her friends.

When they arrived at the cave, they were greeted with a not-so-warm welcome. Many of the elders and members of his tribe were staring at her, as they had not seen any one like her from their colony before. All the members had similar tattoos but with different personal battle marks that glowed in their way. Coming up to the doorway, Trudy noticed that the members of the tribe pulled apart from the middle of the group as a huge wolf walked toward her, thinking that they were giving her as a meal for this wolf, not knowing that this was Elder Nadia, the wisest of all! As this large wolf came closer to Trudy, she began to hear a voice, saying, "Fear not! No harm will come upon you because of the only person that enters on this side of the mountain for only to be chosen." Trudy didn't see the wolf's (Elder Nadia) mouth move but heard her speaking to her loud and clear. She went on telling her she had arrived just in time for the month when they were preparing for their month's feast, and they would love to have her as their special guest to welcome her to this new and blessed world, where people did not know existed.

The evening went on and everybody worked getting ready for the feast. As it was the only time to hunt for food, this gave great enjoyment for everyone to transform (turn to wolf form) and stretch their legs. The tribal family was so happy that someone found them, and this young lady was so beautiful; it would not be hard to find a mate to fall in love with her. With the pleasing God, he would bless this mountain as he promised he would.

The Feast for the New Arrivals

That evening started the monthly feast. One sat at the table with Trudy, and Elder Nadia was sitting at the head of the table. No one could stop gazing at the beauty Trudy held, wondering just who would be the lucky warrior that would have the chance to court the new member of our family. Zax a few wooden stumps down, trying so hard to stand this heartless strong warrior with no feelings as his eyes stayed down staring at his plate. When Elder Nadia felt his presence, she then faced his way. And with a gentle smile, she knew that she had found a match to love Trudy without any help from her. She knew that the two would come together on their own. Once Zax placed aside that warrior image, he would make a great husband and a good dad for the growing tribe.

As Trudy looked around the table, she couldn't help but know that in everything the younger tribe members do, they should acknowledge the wolves first. I didn't know why, but she respected the ways their culture was being carried out. Another way was when every time a meal was placed on their plate, they gave thanks to God as if God himself brought it to their table. After Trudy admired so much beauty of the culture surrounding their meal table, Elder Nadia started telling the history of how and why they did the thing that worked best for their tribe. Why was it so important to give the wolves more respect because of who they were? Trudy couldn't believe what she was hearing. Nadia began by telling of all the powers that the mountain provided, and everyone had a job to do in working together in keeping the life of the mountain going and respecting all the gifts that God gave to us. Elder Nadia told Trudy a lot, but she wasn't allowed to talk about the need for marriage to the tribe also make the mountain expand in the power to bring the population to their culture. As Elder Nadia finished up with the story of their history, it worried Jordon and Trudy's friend Sharon. When Trudy's eyes locked with Sharon's, they ran to each other with such speed, almost knocking each other down. The two friends were so happy to see each other. For a second, they didn't realize that all eyes were on them. At that moment, Elder Nadia didn't realize that there were two women who arrived at their mountain. She (Nadia) foresaw that one young lady might be arriving at the mountain but not two at the same time! Now, with the two young ladies here with the best intention in mind, that's when everyone noticed the walls of the cave started to transform in a way that they hadn't seen before! The running vine began to extend and grow more healing flowers. The water from the well became more forceful when falling into the pond inside the cave, and the markings on everyone's bodies became bolder as their bodies grew. At that moment, the elders knew that all of this was done by the power of God. With all that's just happened in front of their eyes, they all sang and danced more than ever all that night. What a great joy they had witnessed of their God. As the night ended, one of the elders asked Jordon and Zax to show Madam Sharon and Madam Trudy to their sleeping quarters so they could get their proper rest. With no questions, the two warriors escorted the two ladies to their chambers that would take their breath away.

That night, while walking down what seemed to be a cave hallway, the young ladies couldn't help sightseeing like a tourist on vacation for the first time. Sharon wished that she had her camera and a few specimen cups on hand so that she could take some samples back with her to the lab to go into detail on how everything worked around this place. Once they reached the sleeping quarters, Sharon and Trudy stopped in their tracks as they couldn't believe what they were seeing. There in the room was a view like no other. There was a large opening in the wall where you could see the view outside, but the coldness from the mountain was not entering the cave. Small vines were covering the walls and floors. With every step you can feel the energy running up your leg, feeling life itself running throughout the cave. Their resting area (bed) was large and round with a material that looked like some type of moth covered over the bed, like a bird's nest. This made Sharon feel like it was this area (sleeping quarters) for their servants, or was this how they treat their guests? At that time, Zax replied by saying, "Excuse me, madams! I hope you will find the comfort of your likings and rest well," as Zax and Jordon walked backward, with their heads drawn down in respect for the women. When the men pulled close the vine that was covering the cave entrance to their quarters, Trudy turned toward the nest (with the excitement to rest). She then built up speed to jump on the bed of moths. When her body contacted the nest, both ladies were in shock at how the bed was made. This bed was covered in moths but had a soft gel feel underneath but didn't allow their body to get wet. Now Trudy felt this bed. But just when she thought that was all, suddenly a sheer layer of energy covered her bed, like a dome. Sharon, for a second, felt the worse. She was now looking in bed at Trudy, as if she was getting her back massaged. She was then too ready to go to bed. That night, with only Rickey's safety on their mind, the women fell asleep.

Darius's Plans

That night, as the festival was coming to an end, everyone was excited about having a new guest. Started to end with the new blessing of what God might have in store for their tribe's growth. But miles away, as he was standing on a large rock while looking down toward the home of the tribal peoples. As he stood there, his anger was building up by the minute, trying to figure out how and why their God was doing so much for them and not giving his pack the same blessing to turn his pack into human form. Darius then placed his paw on one of the vines (breaking it) to listen in the conversation that the tribal family was having in the cave miles away. Now, knowing that two ladies had arrived at the mountain and knowing what elder Nadia was planning for the young ladies, Darius just couldn't sit back and let that happen! Nadia's family got blessed and grew larger in paradise, and his pack would have to work harder on all fours (legs), while his pack must hunt for their food as his women were unable to bare any kids. Darius gripped his paws on a rock, trying not to start a war the second, to only retrieve his pack in planning to lure the girls away from them to seek revenge.

Now running for miles, reaching the bottom foot of the mountain where Darius's pack lives. This place was not at all a blessed part of the mountain from where Elder Nadia and her tribe lived. This place was always cold; the wind never stopped blowing. Their food was getting harder and harder to come by as the animals themselves tried to reach Maypop Mountain for safety. The trees were always in hibernation all year long, not seeing one leaf on its branches. Everything was grey in color as the wind blew off the key. Not being able to enter his family to the entrance of the Maypop Mountain had Darius not sleeping but only able to think about why their God was not blessing his pack, which made him want to destroy the happiness the Maypop tribe held. Once he gained the power that the mountain would give him to transform into a human. In thinking that he could just possibly cross the forbidden river to the new century civilization. Where he can start a new colony to fill his land where humans and animals will live with no restriction on how they should live, while they have ever-lasting life enjoying the new life. Oh! That was what he thought!

The Next Morning

The next morning, when Sharon and Trudy awakened from their sleep, they were both awoken from their sleep almost at the same moment, as if they were awakened by a time clock. When they opened their eyes in the direction of the other, they both had the biggest smile of comfort on their faces. Trudy noticed that they didn't have the bags under their eyes, a problem that she had suffered with since junior high. Sharon also noticed that her Eshima was all cleared up with events that ever existed. Even the fishy smell was done that the clothes accumulated while fighting for life in the river. Sharon then quickly searched around for whatever she could place in her bag to bring with her to do more research on how it performed in this way of life. After gazing around in the room for things to take, she noticed that everything did not have an ending! The veins ran into the walls, the bed of moths running up from the ground. Just then, she realized that every nature and the tribal people's way of life all came together to make living as a unit.

Come to Zax and Jordon! The only two worriers that patrol the mountain. They announced that they were here by the order of the elders to take Sharon and Trudy around the property to show how the nature functioned, how their cultures tied together, and to show them things that they might convince them to want to stay with them as part of their family. While Trudy tried to find something to make a bag out of for her trip, Sharon then noticed that the markings on Zax's and Jordon's bodies were different from last night. Last night, their marking was goldish in color that glared, as if they had gold flakes on them. The next day, the markings were dark, black in color. She now wanted to pay close attention to these two warriors.

Reaching the last mile before crossing over to unsafe territory where they were forbidden to cross, Jordon began to show Lady Sharon a healing flower. This flower contained so many healing powers:

The smell. When placed under the nose, it would sharpen the eye.

The petals. Drinking it as a tea would repair anything damaged in the body.

The flower. Putting it under the pillow would chases the bad dreams away.

The stem. When placed at the door or opening, bad energy would not enter.

Jordon did not realize just how Sharon's eyes lit up when he showed her this flower, for that was exactly what she came for. She rejoiced in her heart, knowing this flower did exist, trying not to let Jordon realize how happy she was to find such a flower. But she did not know much about the Maypop tribe people, that they all had a gift of telepathy, as he knew exactly what she was here for. The only thing that lingered in his mind was reaching the blessing of his God. So, into the ladies, the young warriors didn't realize that Darius was not far away, watching every move they made, looking for a good time to attack one or all the tribe members. Noticing a bear nearby, Darius decided to visit the bear, for she had something that he wanted the bear to do for him. When he got closer to the bear, Darius then released his sharp claws and dipped them into a sticky glue-like substance. Darius quietly walked to the bear without the bear knowing of his presence and placed his claws into the bear's skin while saying, "Attack the warriors."

The bear was greatly enraged and started charging in the direction of Zax, Jordon, and the two young ladies. When Jordon and Zax realized what's about to happen, they both transformed to attack mode as the ladies ran behind them. Seeing them as true warriors for the first time, not thinking that something they had never seen before was about to happen, Zax and Jordon's body marks became bright gazing gold. Their arms both stood out in attack mode, and that's when the transformation began. They became bigger in size as claws appeared on their hands, while their fur started to grow all over their body. Their faces became longer and more vicious. The girls were thinking about running from them, frightened. As they stood there in attack mode, the warriors then realized the bear was hurt, and it wasn't after them as an enemy. So the warriors attacked the bear, not to hurt him but only to subdue the bear to help treat his wounds.

The girls just stood there, watching everything that was taking place with no words to say. Zax first started changing back to human form, and then Jordon followed. Working together to save the life of the bear, Jordon placed a local flower on the bear's nose to make the bear comfortable so that Zax could drain the poison out of its blood without killing the bear. Recording everything in her mind, Sharon watched every use of the plants the guys used on the bear. Once they finished freeing the bear of the poison, they slowly moved the unconscious bear to a bed of maypop flowers. Placed into the bed of maypop flowers started to glow, and the healing process began on the bear. The two warriors realized that this was the work of Darius, and he was now aware of the young ladies' presence here. Knowing that they must let the elders know of this attack, gripping both ladies by their hands, they rushed them to safety back to the inside of the cave.

Arriving at the entrance of the cave, they were greeted by Elder Nadia, who already knew what just happened, with a huge concern for women's safety. The in-house members came out to the opening to escort the ladies to their rooms so that Elder Nadia and the members of the tribe would have a meeting on how to handle Darius and his pack while staying on track of finding husbands for the young ladies of the blessing that was come upon them by God.

Once entering the meeting room, everyone transformed into war tacks, and the room became soundproof. The surrounding wall became thick with vines and leaves that carried a layer of fiber that becomes soundproof the larger they become, for whatever been told in the meeting room would remain private among those in that room. The mountain placed an invisible shield, covering the door, for any passerby could not even see in that room when walking by!

Elder Nadia began to share her concerns on how they, as a tribe, were so close to receiving their blessing from God! And they couldn't afford Darius to intervene and bring destruction to their land and not think if he reaches the new land of today's humans. It was tragic for their land if humans today knew that their world did exceed. Humans would use all the resources as a quick way to empower each other. This would bring everlasting wars for centuries to come and bring more masters (government) for people today! Then their God would become angry with them over again. That's when warrior Zax replied by saying, "Let's meet with him and give him a peace offering and try to compromise before we start a war and hurt many of our people and Darius's people who mean no harm but are just following Darius's command."

Elder Nadia said, "Well done! We will seek out Darius on a full night to give him a chance to assess our gift and end all rumors of wars to rest."

"But what can we give Darius that has so much value that he wouldn't want to start any wars no more?" replied one of the tribe members.

Once Elder Nadia entered Darius's dream as he lay in a pile of his pack and saw his heart's desire and knew Elder Nadia now knew what would take his mind off wars, Elder Nadia told her tribe to leave it up to her with the gift as she told them (tribe members), to pray to their God to heal Darius's heart and save his wolf pack from death.

Now the night had come to meet Darius and his wolf pack. Elder Nadia told her people that she was going to meet with Darius alone to make sure that her people were safe! But that didn't sit well with everyone. So they decided to travel with her through the underground tunnels so that the wolves wouldn't smell them near to aid Elder Nadia if she got surrounded and needed help from Darius' trickery. As she alerted Darius that she would meet him now at the border of his pack line (the line that they were only allowed to hunt), he (Darius) then called (it was a certain howl that he gave) all his wolves to stop hunting and training for war to come to him so that they all could stand at this meeting so they could prepare to harm the tribe when the time came. So the young, as well as the old, gathered around Darius to discuss war tactics on the tribe. The wolves all let out this powerful howl, signaling war was coming. But they were not aware that the tribal tunnels ran far enough underground to listen to some of the conversations that they were having. This didn't trouble them the slightest about what the wolves were planning to do.

That night at the meeting, Elder Nadia stood graceful in her canary yellow dress with gems and gold traveling down her dress, as if it was telling a story as it shimmered under the full moon to ensure Darius that she didn't come for war but to gather understanding and place differences away so that all could live together in peace, that way by passing her safety line on to territory signaling to him that she means no harm to him and his wolves. Darius did not know about the underground tunnels with her tribe, ready to attack on the first sign of fear from Elder Nadia. Darius approached, noticing that she came alone and didn't sit well with him, knowing that her people were somewhere around and ready for a fight as were his people. Before Madam Nadia started to speak, Darius couldn't help but notice her beauty. There she stood upright with such grace and a perfect pose, while he knew that she could shift in any given second. He could also see the power flowing in her dress, just waiting to be used at any given second on them during the war. But in Darius's heart knows with his large pack, he would still be outnumbered without the power that the tribe carried with them. Now Darius was interested in what Elder Nadia ha to say!

Now Madam Nadia started to speak, her dress gently changed color from canary yellow to a cool blue, the signal to her people that Darius had come down, and he was now ready to listen to what she had to say! Nadia started explaining to Darius the reason for the borderline was because he took lives for hunger and that the tribal borderline was to keep the population of life going throughout the mountain. Without life renewing itself, life on this mountain would not exist, and it was not good to let his pack run free around the woods because they would harm the plant life. The plants were so important that they brought so much life to their people and healed sick animals and the water all around this mountain. That's why it was so important to Maypop Mountain. Elder Nadia knew that Darius and his pack were not getting their hands on the power the mountain held. That's when she raised her hand to offer him a gift that would stop him from calling off the war. In her hand that she held up to Darius was a canister with a glowing liquid in it. Nadia leaned closer and whispered words into it, and then the liquid seemed to come to life. She stepped up to Darius and handed it down at his feet. Madam Nadia told him that this was a gift to him from her and her tribe if he would not harm her people and their land at any time anymore. She went on by saying that "as long you don't harm the people and the animals of the Maypop Mountain, every full moon, the liquid will refill itself in this canister. This canister is filled with wishes if you are on your land. One person can become a human for a day, can heal any of their sick packs, and can pour the liquid on a stone, and they will have an abundance of food your pack can feast on without harming any animals on this mountain. Pour the liquid around your pack on the coldest nights. It will bring you warmth throughout the night." With another warning to Darius, she spoke to him again, saying, "You must not use this in any way to harm, for this liquid will not renew itself."

Darius accepted the gracious gift. But back in his mind, thinking like a wolf, it must be somewhere over in the mountain cave, so they did not have to obey Nadia's rules. Darius opened his mouth, grabbed the gift, turned around, and began to head to the woods, as if the pack was going to fall. He then looked at one of the second wolves to command to start what they came here to do!

That's when Ty (second-in-charge) started howling and jumping fearlessly at Elder Nadia. As Ty was in the air, coming in Nadia's direction angrily, Nadia's dress turned into a red battle suit of arms. Her crown changed into a face shield, and her dress became hard and broke up into parts to cover her body, protecting every inch of her and thickening itself to protect her body! Before Ty's paws touched the ground, the tribe warriors were coming out of the ground in a powerful force. As they rose out of the ground, they were transforming into a very large and very powerful beast of war. As the transformation was done, and their paws hit the ground, they all gathered around Nadia for her safety, giving the wolves a second chance to decide if war was what they wanted to do. Darius was nowhere to be found and only caring about himself, leaving his pack, thinking that this would be an equal fight between the two enemies. Darius was thinking, the fighting going on would give him time to drink the magic liquid as he crossed the river, and he would become permanently human so he could walk among the new-century people as a human. Meanwhile, Darius's pack was not aware of his plans and was now facing sudden death from the war with the tribe. As warriors, Zax and Jordon took the lead in the fighting on the tribe's behalf. With their quick hands and thinking, every time a wolf leaped at one of them, they were always a step ahead of the wild wolves' reaction. With the tribal wolves' grip, they ripped Darius's wolf pack apart, leaving them helpless and waiting to die.

Looking down at the devastation, Elder Nadia raised her, as if she had enough of the useless war. Just then, Zax and Jordon released the remaining wolves from their grip. The remaining wild wolves retrieved by running, and some limped back into the woods to recover from their ordeal, thinking that Darius would be waiting on them to drink the liquid to heal them from their war wounds. The wolves that lost their lives on the fighting ground would now be fed on by bears and the mountain lions throughout the winter.

Jordon and Zax, still in war formation, walked toward Elder Nadia, as if she was ready to give them a new order to find Darius. With the power of telepathy, she knew of his whereabouts and of Darius's plans with the magic potion in his hands. They all knew that if Darius reached the other side, he could let others know that they were real, and people around would try to find them for their land and medicine. That would become dangerous if the secret was released. So she ordered the warrior to find him and take the potion from him. Jordon and Zax, along with two other warriors, sat out to retrieve Darius and the potion before he had a chance to wreak havoc on the new generation of humans with their nose raised to pick up Darius's scent. Darius was smart enough to use some of the potions to give him some time to getaway, knowing that they would come looking for him at some point in time. Not picking up Darius's scent made it harder to know which direction of the river he might be at. That's when Jordon went to an area on the river and placed his paw in the water to speak to the fish by sending a sonic signal to the them to make it hard to cross for anybody. In an instant, the water became rough, like rough tides during a storm out at sea. This was a very good plan to give them time to reach Darius before he crossed the river with the potion.

Honoring the
School Mission

Now Sharon and Trudy grew tired of waiting for everyone to return from their emergency security breach, waiting for what seemed like a very long time with one of the tribe members called Ms. Mae. Ms. Mae worked very hard on keeping the young ladies entertained by showing them all the carvings and how the jewels came from all over the walls and what vines would make the best medicines. The ladies were so thankful for what the cave had to offer, but their heart was craving to explore what was going on all around the mountain. So while traveling down a long tunnel, the girls saw that the tunnel began to break apart in serval different ways and decided to quietly take one piece of the tunnel without Ms. Mae knowing, in search for a way out of the cave, to search for the proof of good evidence to take with them to show the school that the Maypop Mountain was real.

As the young ladies traveled down a dark hallway, they noticed that the jewels were not lighting up for them, which made walking more difficult, not knowing where to step as there was running water getting very close to them. But the temptation of what they might find once they reached outside life and what they might discover on their own. Sharon grabbed Trudy's hand as they continued to walk in the dark. While they were walking, the young ladies noticed that they were walking alongside running water. In just a blink of an eye, Sharon lost her footing and slid into the water. Trudy was struggling to stay afloat so she could hear Sharon's voice and grab her hand, screaming for help from anyone nearby to pull her and help her pull Sharon out of the water because the rocks were too slippery. Just then, a bright glow grew in the water, and the dark tunnel began to light up with the gems on the walls. Trudy now was able to see Sharon very well! But she then realized that she wasn't alone anymore. There swimming beside Sharon was the most beautiful person, helping Sharon onto the edge of the tunnel to safety! She didn't say anything but smiled. Trudy couldn't help Sharon out of the water because the beauty of that person just wouldn't let her take her eyes off the lady in the water. The colors that recoiled her from the smiling lady were as if slow dancing to a Gerald LeVert song. That's when Sharon realized that the lady had a tail, like a fish. This was a real live mermaid, swimming right in front of them. That's when Ms. Mae walked up and said, "Oh! I see you have met our sea family!"

That's when Ms. Mae waved at the mermaid, and then she swam away. Then Ms. Mae looked at the two young ladies and said, "You need to out the Maypop Mountain." That's when she walked the young energetic ladies out to the safe side of the mountain, where she knew they would be far away from danger. Walking to the end of the tunnel, they started to see light, and the opening had the most intense sweet smell. They just had to see where the smell was coming from. And when they arrived, there were so many colorful flowers. The flowers were all running on a vine, and the vines had lights running throughout each flower, as if it was electricity running through a cord. That's when Ms. Mae began to tell them the story of this flower called the maypop flower. She started telling them how they first arrived and that they were cold with nothing to eat, while some of them were ill and very weak! The first fruit-like plant was this maypop plant that they saw. Desperate for food, and they didn't arrive with anything to hunt with, the kids cried as their stomachs hurt from tiredness and hunger. It was up to the elders to take a chance to test out this unknown fruit that seemed abundant on this side of the mountain.

So Elder Nadia was the first one to try the maypop fruit so she would know of the side effects of the foods and medicines while living on the plantation. Elder Nadia looked back, holding the fruit in front everyone standing together, shivering cold and hungry, leaving no choice but to take a bite of the fruit in order people. Once she took a bite, Ms. Nadia just stood very still, focused, the hard pain or illness coming on. But within a minute, she started feeling a fullness in her stomach, and the cuts that she accumulated on herself in the woods started to heal. Elder Nadia noticed that the cold weather didn't bother her anymore. She then didn't hesitate to give the fruit to eat. After an hour, she checked to see if anybody was affected by the fruit, only to see they all came to life with more strength and feeling full, as if they just finished a Thanksgiving meal. She saw everyone coming to life, as they did on the plantation on a holiday.

She knew right then that this was the new Jerusalem for them. The will of God spared their life and gave them a new world and a new name. It took them to arrive at the opening of the cave when we knew that our lives would not be the same anymore. That is when writings began to appear on the sparkly wall, welcoming them here and telling them all about the powers of the cave. Even though they had never been to school, they understood very well the writings on the wall. The last sentence said not to be afraid but to be blessed, coming from the century of chains to become great and very powerful warriors. At that moment, the older adults started to transform into wolves, as the writing on the wall said, "Here, accept the transformation, for the elder was closer to death's door and now is immortal and will live forever as long as they shelter on this side of the mountain. They are now the head (the leaders) of this blessed place." It also had a message for younger men and women: "The young men are needed as warriors, guarding the grounds and keeping the family and the animals safe, only allowing good animals to cross the borders onto our land. For the young ladies, keep every living thing and everyone healthy. If the flower starts to wither, the mountain has living water. If the animal feels ill, I have planets to heal them. If a human feels not their best, I give you beds that take the problem away." That was when Sharon decided that when she got back home, she would be writing a novel about this amazing place. This place seemed like the new Eden for God's new generation of his people.

When Two Join

While Zax and Jordon searched all the crossing points of the river, even with the help of the river friends (mermaids), they couldn't locate Darius anywhere. With the ability of telepathy, Jordon and Zax sensed that Darius was out of harm's way. So they decided to head back to the cave and stay on the lookout for any activity of Darius's mischievous behavior around the mountain, not think that Darius still had the magic potion and that all along, Darius was under their nose with a shield surrounding him to camouflage him and to throw, everyone even his pack, off his track until he got a chance to make a clean getaway! Now back at the cave, the young warriors were still in transformation as a wolf, not thinking of the new visitors that were waiting in the cave, startling the young ladies while still in their wolf formation. The girls screamed as Sharon grabbed a war stuff from the wall, and Trudy hid behind her in fear. With the mean (angry) expressions on their faces, their broad bodies glowed with blazing streaks of gold. Sharon and Trudy were not aware that they were Jax and Jordon. They just walk past the young ladies without any care of going to battle with the women. So the ladies decided to follow the wolves to see where they were going! The warriors led them down a hall that they were not former with to a room that looked like their sleeping quarter. The warriors each lay on a bed of glowing leave, and then they closed their eyes. Then vines covered all over them as they rest on the bed of leaves. The vines gave a soft purple glow, and there the wolves just lay, as if they were in a spa. Then the vines stopped glowing and started to crawl back to where it came from. At that moment, they realized it was Jordon and Zax. When the guys opened their eyes, they just gazed at the young ladies, as if they knew all about them all along.

Now Elder Nadia graciously stepped in front of them (Sharon, Trudy, Jordon, and Zax) with a humble smile, telling them that she had a task for them: to help her find this root for the upcoming ceremonial celebration. So she sent Sharon and Jordon out to retrieve a root that would rapidly grow anything that it encountered, not really needing this root, but this would give Sharon and Jordon time to get to know each other. With the spiritual wisdom that Nadia had, it led her to unite Sharon with Jordon in bringing joy to the tribe, while Sharon was not aware of the blessings that the tribe would have in her honor. To become blessed, they must fall in love naturally, and Sharon was unaware of the truth. There they started. Sharon threw her satchel across her chest and gathered her tools. Jordon, being a young warrior, only picked up his battle staff and his shield. Jordon was only thinking about Darius's locations. They both started walking in the direction of where they would find the root that Elder Nadia needed for the ceremony. With Sharon so fascinated with science, Elder Nadia knew that the way to the rocky cave, where the root was located, would keep Sharon full of excitement to get to know the soft side of Jordon.

As they walked out of sight, Elder Nadia faced Trudy and Zax and gave them a warm smile. Then she began to tell them that she needed the bark from a tree for protection. This tree had a gift that no other tree offered. When you retrieve the bark from this tree and hold it close to your body, it would cover a shield around you for protection. You would be able to use the bark only once before the life force would be drawn out of it. Trudy bowed in front of Elder Nadia with such grace, as if she was a foreign princess of a country.

When Trudy finished bowing her head, the sun captured her eyes for a moment, taking both Nadia's and Zax's breaths by her great beauty, just coming from Trudy's eyes alone. Elder Nadia looked at Zax to see if the princess had arrived. That's when Elder Nadia said to Zax, "Go and find the tree bark and then show her the powers it can perform."

Not having a bag on hand, Trudy searched for areas on Zax and herself to place any object on their body so that they could bring back the bark from what Elder Nadia asked of them to retrieve. So Trudy and Zax started on their journey to bring back the bark for the ceremony. When they started traveling, both did not know how to start a conversation until Turdy noticed all the flowers and shrubs swaying over as they passed them by in the woods, as well as how their glow became brighter, as if they gave them light as them walk. Zax noticed how Trudy was admiring her surroundings and felt the need to tell her how everything and everyone that lived here work to help each other in nature's ring of life. He also went on about how life here survived on God's blessings. With his blessing, they came to think of this as the new Eden that was once foretold in the Bible that they once read while growing up on the plantation where he once was a toddler. But over here, everyone and everything would not live in bondage.

Zax was so into his words that he didn't realize that Trudy was noticing the markings on his body began to glow a shimmering gold. As curious as Trudy was, she just took a step back and allowed Zax to continue to explain life here. Zax then noticed how Trudy was watching him instead of listening to what he was saying. That's when he looked down and saw that she was watching his glowing body. Now instead of asking questions about the flowers, Trudy was ready to ask questions about him and the truth behind this tribe. Not knowing where to start telling her and what he could tell her without letting her in on the blessing for the reason of their arrival, while traveling on a distant trail, Zax started reaching over and placing flowers and herbs into Trudy's hand, telling her that she would be using this for later. He began to speak about life on the plantation. Zax was very young, and he talked about what he could remember because as a young boy, the elders tried to shield the kids from all the bad things that went on the plantation. As he could remember, this owner wasn't like the townspeople. They (white folks) were so mean and did great harm to the people of color. They soon brought in smaller people with cat eyes to our town, but they couldn't speak their language. But they took them to make and lay down heavy metal on the ground. Their owner was a kind man; he wasn't like the townspeople, mean to his workers. He was a believer in God's words, and his words were always preached on greatness among his people. When no visitors were meeting their owner at his home that day, he let them sing and dance the whole day if all their chores were done, and all the animals were fed. But on a later summer night, his life ended, and not even Elder Nadia's medicine could heal him from death. The following week, they were to be sold in the town's auction. Of all the families that were on the plantation, their family was the only one that didn't want to take a chance of having the worse owner, and all their lives would be changed forever. That was when his family prepared to escape to the forbidden mountain that the local people were all scared to travel to because of the legend of the old, white witch. During their travel, they even met the witch in the woods, and she gave them safe travel and told them how to cross the river. Once they arrived, there was no doubt in their minds that it truly was a greater power that brought them this far. The presence of God here on this land led them to work together along with the animals to heal and preserve their land and to keep it a secret.

Just then, Zax stopped talking and told Trudy that they were here! Trudy stopped and looked to the top of the tree, as if the tree was never going to stop (that's just how tall they were). Three trees were standing over 200 ft. This tree was so massive that the bark on this tree was all in a sequence of patterns. Even though these trees weren't glowing, the greenery coming from them, as well as the diameter of these trees, you could tell that it had been around for centuries. That's when she came in for a closer look and saw that life was working on one of the trees. It was a colony of ants. They saw that they were harvesting the sap from the tree, and some of the ants looked like they were giving something back to the tree. Trudy was amazed at what she saw. That is when Zax bowed in front of the ants and softly blew on the ants. Right then, the ants parted ways for Zax but never stopped working. So Zax reached his hand over to the tree and pulled off four pieces of bark from the tree. When Zax placed the bark in Trudy's hand, that is when he gave thanks to the tree by placing his hand on the tree and chanting soft words to it. Once Zax opened his eyes, he looked at Trudy and said in a friendly voice, "It's still early. Let me show you something."

Instead of heading back to the cave, Zax and Trudy took the path behind the trees, where you could hear running water. Walking about twenty minutes, they came to another part of the river that Trudy hadn't seen before. This river was pouring itself into a large lake. With all the rushing of water, once it poured into the lake, the water became very calm. The water was crystal clear that you could see the colors bouncing from the rocks at the bottom of the lake. There were so many fish that once you place your hand in the water, they didn't run away but had so much curiosity to meet you. Just when Trudy looked up, Zax was standing over her with a piece of bark in hand. He told her to place the bark in her mouth and to stay calm. That's when Zax held her hand and reassured Trudy that she would be amazed at what he was about to show her. As he pulled her into the water, Trudy quickly remembered that arriving at Maypop Mountain was not an easy experience here! So she started to pull back from the water. Once the water had reached their waist, and their teeth still gripping the back that was in their mouth, a sheer shield came, surrounding their head. As Zax and Trudy finally admire underwater, Trudy started to put up a fight with the water, thinking that he might try to drown her for sacrifice as she tried to swim back to the shore. Zax finally got her to calm down, and then he placed his hand behind her ear. Without his mouth moving he began to speak to her, and she was so surprised to hear and understand him very well. With the security she felt with Zax, Trudy then calmed down and noticed that she was underwater. And with the help of the shield covering her head, she was able to breathe. She excitedly explored the beautiful scenery of the corals and all kinds of curious fish she was happy to meet. Some followed them while giving them the lighting that they needed as they traveled deeper into the water. On their way to swim around this huge boulder, we can up to two tall columns that look like there once was a door entering a hold new place under the sea. That's when she saw all of them (a family of mermaids), swimming up to her with the biggest smiles on their faces. As Trudy held on to Zax's hand tighter, that's when one young mermaid came up to Trudy, with a necklace placed around her neck and saying, "Welcome. They have been waiting for her to arrive." Unable to smile, Trudy's eyes grew wider than ever, with great joy at seeing this for the first time. The other mermaids motioned for them (Trudy and Zax) to follow them to show her many interesting views and their culture underwater. As their time was coming to an end, many of the mermaids honored Trudy with a bag of gifts and underwater plants and told the tribe to tell her the meaning of all the things that she had in her bag. They also told her to serve these things with a purpose and not to do harm with the items that they gave to her. That's when Zax and Trudy bid them farewell and started to swim back to the surface while caring for the gifts that were given to her.

Now when Sharon and Jordon arrive at the cave to find the plant that Elder Nadia needed for the ceremony, there wasn't much of a conversation going on, for Sharon feared Jordon becoming angry and changing into a wolf and hurting her. Jordon then placed his hand in front of Sharon to stop her from entering the dark cave. He also told her that he would enter first due to the loose rocks and that she might hurt herself. Jordon entered and walked a few feet and turned to signal to Sharon that it was all clear to enter. This cave didn't have all the glamour of lights as the Maypop Mountain. This cave was on the borderline, where a few yards Darius's pack resides.

While they walked farther down into the cave where they believed the plants were housed, Jordon knew how Sharon was intrigued by the new surroundings, and he had to mention to her that whatever she would take from the cave, she must give something back as an offering. The belief of this cave was to always keep a balance. So if you took something, you had to replace it to keep the balance of nature. When Sharon and Jordon came to the waterfall, and the light came from the outside, there running down the sides of the waterfall was the plant that they came here for. Jordon told her to take as much as she needed and nothing else. So Sharon did just that, and they both started to walk back out of the cave to get Elder Nadia the flower that she needed for the ceremony. But on the way back, Sharon spotted some small mushrooms that looked like small gummy candies of all colors, standing in a patch all over the cold and damp area in the cave. She asked Jordon what they were, and Jordon answered her, saying that the mushrooms were not to be touched because of the poison that it had inside. It would first make you very strong before you become very ill and sometimes die. That's when Jordon walked away from the mushroom and left the cave. Sharon couldn't help herself by placing a cloth over the mushroom so that she wouldn't come in contact to make her sick so that she could take the mushroom back for more studying of this plant.

With Jordon walking in and Sharon coming up on the rear, leaving the cave, that is when things started to happen. Sharon forgot the rule of the cave: "You take something from the cave; you will have to leave something behind as an offering," which she forgot to do. Just before they were to be cleared from the doorway of the cave, the wind became wild and came out of knowledge. The trees started to sway badly, and the rock became unstable, tossing them both back into the cave. While so much was going on, and Jordon was calling to Sharon to give something back to the cave, one of the plants rolled out of her bag. At that moment, everything stopped, trapping her feet in between two stones and Jordon's body being trampled on with falling rocks from the cave. Jordon was lying on the ground, trying to get his breath while asking Sharon if she was okay. With the scream coming from her area, she didn't hear him calling her. There Sharon's leg got stuck in between two rocks. Jordon stumbles over to help her from the rock, but he couldn't raise the rock in his human form. That's when Jordon closed his eyes, then his breathing got heavy, and that's when Sharon started to see the transformation (turning into the wolf) once again. Due to all the pain that she was feeling, Sharon fainted, not noticing Jordon as a fully formed wolf and seeing how he pulled apart two large stones to remove her leg from danger.

While Sharon was still unconscious, Jordon was able to transform back to human form to carry her out of the cave and render aid to her wounds. Jordon ran into the woods, as Sharon lay near the cave, to retrieve the nearest maypop plant to heal Sharon's injury. There he knelt beside her and crushed the flower into a paste and applied it to her injury. While the crushed plant lay on her skin, the glow got dimmer as the medicine traveled to Sharon's body and continued to heal her. Sharon began to open her eyes and only said that she was sorry for taking the mushroom that caused the cave to collapse. Knowing that he couldn't afford to be angry with her after what just happened, Jordon just said in a calm voice, "It was an old and abandoned cave anyway." So they decided to stay and make a fire there until Sharon was strong enough to walk back to the tribe's cave. Feeling better by the minute, Sharon began to tell Jordon about all the amazing things that went on at the university, how people from all walks of life lived and worked with each other. There was no slavery. Everyone went to school and could become doctors and own their stores. Even the people of color could own their stores. The look in Jordon's eyes was so amazing, knowing that the new-generation world had changed so much.

Darius's Chance

Now Darius lay under a neighboring tree with a sheered force field hind him away from the Maypop tribe and also this pack. As Darius lay there, he couldn't help but think that walking away from this pack would be the right thing to do! Or just a chance to reach the new generation land in order to become immortal and take a chance on life as a human. Once he crossed the lake, he then would be able to prove to his belated parents that he would prove to the pack that the three hope for immortality for them. Because growing up as a cub always felt that having three lives in the woods were greater than just hunting for food and training for war that never came.

Growing up as a cub, Darius always wanted to become great. Living with a pack before the tribe arrived at the Maypop Mountain, the wolf pack lived where everyone hunted and slept as a group. This didn't suit young Darius very well because this young cub had a very strong imagination of how his future would become for him. As Darius sometimes listened to his grandfather (Papa Frank), sitting around one of the hot steams that came out of the hole slowly as it kept them warm throughout the night and after a good meal that their parents had gathered up earlier that day, Papa Frank would always tell the young cubs stories of magic worlds. His papa shared with them stories years before when he himself was a cud.

He began telling them of a place where food would be abundant; you wouldn't have to hunt for food but only to have food and seasoning at your paw reach, how the creatures walked on two legs, and there were some that wore flashy attire with things that shine around their necks and on their heads. They had people working for them, and they always bowed at their feet. Darius would stare at his grandfather for hours as he would tell how one day a few would cross the river and change their lives forever. Papa even went on saying how there would become a time where wolves would be able to transform into humans. At that moment, Darius admittedly knew that his life was destined for that greatness. Darius knew then that he had to gather up as much knowledge to become the tribe king whenever they arrive. Once he took over the tribe's magic and power, then Darius would be able to travel to the new world to become even greater, with the power, riches, and resources to take over the new world. That night, Grandpapa was finishing up his stories for the night. Darius's best friend, Dallas, born just days after Darius, they became very close throughout the years. Dallas would always seem to keep Darius out of trouble. The two were inseparable, so they learned how to hunt and discover the life of the mountain. Many years had passed, and Darius and Dallas were now teens and didn't realize that their parents had planned their arrange marriage to each other on the first day of adulthood. When the two heard the news, it didn't really bother them because they were the best of friends. Darius would go on for hours talking about how he would rule the mountain with Dallas alongside him.

Until one day, the pair (Dallas and Darius) wanted to climb this particular tree. It was once said that if you climb this tree, you would be able to see the new world. And if you look even harder, you might even get a chance to see machines in the air and houses that reached the sky. So one day, Darius and Dallas had this bright idea to climb to the top, hoping for a glance of the new world and the people that were over there and the machines that dwelled in the presence of the humans that he might take over someday. Finally making it to the tree, Darius gave Dallas a lift to an old tree that had fallen years ago that was lying against the tree that would carry them to reach the tree to look over to the new world. Now walking and jumping from tree to tree with loud laughter and joking as good friends do, they had reached the safest part of the tree. Darius and Dallas still couldn't see any signs of the new world. But wait, something was going on from afar that seemed like movement. They had to get closer to take a better look of what was going on over there. The branch that they needed for a better view didn't support Darius's weight. Dallas told him that she was lighter than him, so it would be better if she went out there and told him all that she saw. So both agreed. Dallas, with a big smile, stared slowly, crawling out there on the branch. As she reached the middle of the branch with the excitement of what she seeing and a continent, reminding Darius of what he was missing. The view and the things that she was describing to him seemed so breathtaking; it made him want to run up there. But the tree wouldn't carry their weight together.

That moment, time stood still, and Dallas looked at Darius to make fun at him. Not able to get the last word out, the branch gave way, and Dallas disappeared, falling down out of the tree on the downside of the mountain where no one was able to look over to see if she was able to hold on for them to come and rescue her. Once Darius came down out of the tree, he looked at the side of the mountain, calling her name repeatedly, but there was no answer. When Darius finally reached the pack, he told the older wolves and her parents what had happened, and they all ran in the direction where she had fallen. Following Dallas's sent to her whereabouts, they discovered a lifeless body of a female wolf, lying on the ground. Every one of the packs started howling as a custom of the pack when a wolf died. Weeks after the Dallas's ceremony, Darius lay in a small cave, where only he could fit. He lay for days, blaming himself of Dallas's death. His parents stood at cave's opening, not able to fit in, trying to get Darius to come back to the pack. Still Darius didn't comply. He just held his head under his paw, as if his parents weren't outside of the cave. After months, one morning, Darius came out of the cave, looking very thin over the weight he lost. They (the pack) noticed something was off about him. Darius's heart became cold, and he lost all reason to smile and join in the for fun and hunting. Until one day, he just left without anyone in the pack knowing and didn't hear from him anymore.

Years later, as Darius had grown up with the west pack, he started hearing rumors of newcomers arriving to the mountain. They began to say that the mountain came to life, and everything was in abundance. This made Darius think about all that his papa told him years ago when he was just a cub. They even told him how they arrived home, looking sick and weakened. But a few wolves witnessed the miracle of God, blessing them with great powers and poured out much blessing to the rivers and the northern forest where they lived. The rivers became glowing with plenty of fish, as they were seen jumping in and out of the water. Plants grew bigger and thicker with the sparkle of life traveling throughout the vines of the plants. The animals were seen traveling in larger groups, and everyone and everything had more happiness of life.

The Celebration

Arriving back at the cave from a life-threatening ordeal, both Sharon and Trudy were ordered to go back to their rooms and take a rest and when they wake, to get dressed, for tonight they would be celebrating their arrival with a great feast and music and dancing. But she really wanted to tell them that the celebration was for the announcement of engagement of both couples or one couple. All the tribe needed was one to grant the blessing from the heavens, but very love if both of the young ladies become the wives of the favorable warriors. The bearing of a new generation would be exactly what the tribe needed to start having a little one running around and learning the goodness of God's wonderful works, the joy of seeing God's blessing growing in front of their eyes. The land would widen as the flying birds to the fireflies flying around with thinking lights as if it was singing song from the heavens all night to the wee hours of the night. The flowers would send out sweet smell of perfume to send their love to the All-High as everyone breathed in to the great smell from the flower that God had made. Even the fish in the river would serenade, with flashes of colors coming out of the river, serving as happiness to welcome the new blessing. The trees would sway back and forth, as if it was an audience, clapping softly, welcoming the celebration.

When Sharon and Trudy awakened from their nap, they were greeted with the most beautiful dresses hanging right in front of their beds. The ladies' dresses were designed with so many details that seemed that the dresses were made long before their arrival. The beads were so detailed that the dresses were telling a story by themselves. The jewelry (stones) on the dresses made them sparkle so gracefully, as if they were only made for the royal princess. They both were so excited about trying on the dresses for tonight and to dance the night away in the festival tonight. Once Sharon placed on her dress, her first thought was how to take all of the blessed tokens (the finding and artifacts), to place all her objects to her college for all to see, and for them to believe her that this place was real. Her school would have more accreditations for more discovery of new places.

When Trudy tried on her dress, she at an instant felt like the most beautiful princess and the way the dress took on a glow, as if the dress was waiting to put it on. Once the dress settled on her body, the vines on the dress started growing on as it ran down her arm and across her neck, like jewelry fit for a princess. Flakes of gold began to fall from the ceiling onto her hair, as if she was the honoree for the night.

Trudy and Sharon began staring at each other in great surprise just before they both burst with laughter as they turned around, admiring their dress. Now came a gentle knock on the room entrance, and a soft voice said to them that everyone was expecting them in the main dining area. While the ladies both were walking to the dining area, they noticed that the walls of the caves glowed much brighter than before. Reaching the entrance of the dining area, they were greeted by a few elder wolves, gracefully bowing as the ladies walked past the celebration. They now realized that this party was for them. Now, at the celebration, two tall gentlemen stood in front of them with their best soldier uniform, standing as if they were their host for the night. Zax and Jordon reached out and took the hands of the young ladies and led them to the center of the dance floor. Once at the center of the floor, both men held the young ladies. They felt a sense of closeness toward the young men. Both Trudy and Sharon admittedly knew that they were now the center of the plan all along. But at that moment, the two girls, facing the soldiers' chests, danced as if it was the last night before they returned home.

Sharon didn't know how to tell them that she didn't want to stay, but all she wanted was to take her finds and return them to her school. Not to mess up a beautiful night, Sharon promised to have a talk to the elder mother the next morning about leaving to preside over her career. But for Trudy, her feeling was so trapped, casing into Zax eyes that she forgot her mission and even not thinking of Ricky, waiting three days on the other side of the river, waiting for them to help them to cross safety. With a soft smile, Trudy felt as if this was a place that she had been in her dream that was calling to her to come and never knew what it meant to her until now!

After the music ended, Elder Nadia stood up from the table and said for everyone to raise their glasses to welcome their new and only guests. Elder Nadia began saying to the young ladies, "There has been a prophecy on your arrival. And the only way it can come to pass is to agree to accept God's blessing for the tribe," meaning a surprised marriage to one of her available soldiers. She also began to say that they would not be forced to stay and to marry. But on returning to the new world, all of the memories would be erased to protect this magical place. Not waiting for an answer now but in the morning when they all awakened, they could come to her with an answer of our decision. Now Sharon and Trudy would have to break the news about returning to the school and ask for permission to return with the plants and the finds to take back with them.

The next morning, both girls didn't sleep a wink, as Sharon thought of how she could take the items back and make a name for herself. Trudy couldn't sleep, thinking that she really loved being around Zax, and this place was so amazing that she really felt like she belonged here! But her mission was for the sac of the collage, and she couldn't let the college down from her findings in this magical land. A knock came to the cave open door, and once again, a soft voice said to the young ladies that the elder wanted to see them now! The two glanced at each other and took a deep breath to prepare themselves to break the bad news on returning home.

Decision Day

Walking in the corridor with the vision of Elder Nadia, both of the young ladies took a deep breath, knowing what their answer was for Elder Nadia. Nadia, with the gift of sight, knew the answer already but gave the young ladies a chance to change their minds on leaving with nothing or staying to live like two princesses living in paradise. Now she asked the two young ladies on their decision to stay. First it was Sharon to answer, and she started by saying, "Madam, this place is too beautiful with many riches of minerals to save many people's lives. And the gold and the jewels will bring wealth to our government." Nadia, standing there with such grace while keeping calm on their decision, was thinking about not retrieving the blessing from God. But all hope was not lost when it came to Trudy! Sensing Trudy's heart grew in emotion wanting to do the right thing, but have to keep her reason why they came in the first place for the life of the school. But when she looked over to Zax's eyes, she knew that he didn't want her to leave because his feelings for her in his heart was so great. Then both Sharon and Trudy came to an agreement to do what was best for their school and to go back in hoping that Madam Nadia wouldn't take all their memory from them so that they could bear witness of all of their findings of the Maypop Mountain. Elder Nadia asked Zax and Jordon to escort the ladies down to the river, where there was a boat waiting for them to give them safe travel back across the river.

Jordon, who really hadn't said anything about diction making of the tribe, he really enjoyed the idea of having a mate and wanted to become a part of helping to retrieving the blessing from God. This would bring so much happiness to the tribe with the joy of populating the mountain with the voices of baby's laugher around the mountain. Even the time to have a family of his own excited him. But the feeling and the time he spent with Sharon was so comforting having her by his side with the feeling of a friend with laughter and not having war on this mind on daily bases. Even though Sharon didn't have the power to shift and had no magical ability that Jordon had, In know the blessing of the mountain, God would work it out so that their unity would be a blessed one. While escorting the ladies down to the river, wanting so desperately to change Sharon's mind, he knew that he couldn't make or speak of the gift to come. So he just continued to softly talk to her as they walked down to the river to bid her farewell.

Trudy had so many questions of what would happen if she stayed and not to return to their world, questions like, Would she be the only one to grow old? Or would she be able to leave when she feels like her time had come to go home? Then Elder Nadia started by saying to her, "Yes! And yes!" Elder Nadia continued to say! "We here at the Maypop Mountain have so many blessings on our land that we don't need to hold anyone here on our land. Our land chooses the people to come to the mountain. Our tribe just welcomes everyone with open arms." Trudy was still undecided to stay, but her heart didn't want to leave this beautiful paradise. Trudy also remembered that when she was studying at the school, she didn't have many friends because she was always focused on her studies. And growing up as the only child, she didn't get the joy with in a group called a family. Trudy enjoyed the closeness of the tribe's family as lone with the study of what the mountain had to offer.

They now arrived at the boat, a small but sturdy boat with a few fruits, just in case the girls get hungry on their way back to the new world. The boat was held by two mermaids, smiling as they loved to see Sharon and Trudy. The first one who entered the boat was Sharon as she said her short goodbyes because her mind was really about getting back home with all the information and that the artifacts of the existing journey were real. But before Trudy could step onto the boat, Jordon walked up to Madam Nadia and started talking to her by saying, "Mama! May I ask of you to give Sharon a little of the memory to take back with her to bear witness but not a sense of direction on how to return back to the mountain?" Then Jordon also said to Elder Nadia, "Let her go back with Sharon and learn the ways of life with the new-generation people and to be able to come back to the mountain to learn our people how different life have changed since they have been sense they living on the mountain."

Then Elder Nadia's eyes grew wider since that was a great idea to know what going on in the new world. She (Nadia) noted and said, "I will give you this because when you arrived here to the Maypop Mountain, you and Jordon were very young and didn't know the plantation while with the surrounding people. So, yes! You shall go and return in three moons. Take in all the information to bring back to learn us of the new generation ways and how many culture of peoples and are they still in bondage with the government." She also told Jordon that he would be the only one to travel back to them. Jordon then noted and said, "Yes, ma'am," and bowed at her and turned to step in the boat.

Just when Trudy turned to step in, at that moment, Zax grabbed Trudy by the hand to bid her to stay. As Trudy was trying to tell him that she had to return back while he was pulling her out the boat, her heart and her feet were guiding her out the boat, leaving Sharon and Jordon sitting in the boat, wondering why she (Trudy) needed to stay in this world. Now Nadia nodded to the mermaids to start the boat to set sail with only Sharon and Jordon in the boat. But at the edge of the lake, there was Zax, holding Trudy in his arms as her feet dangled off the ground because of his height. There Trudy knew that she was in the right place of her life, as she waved goodbye to her best friend, not knowing if she would ever see her again in this life. When the boat was at a great distance, Madam Nadia then turned to return to the cave to wait on God's instructions on the blessing to come.

Miles down the river, the mermaids came to the end of escorting the boat in the direction of where it needed to travel to reach a safe opening, where Ricky awaited by the river for the girls' safety. While Jordon was trying to hold back his excitement of seeing a new world by making conversations with Sharon, Sharon was wondering what she would tell them of what happen to Trudy. The hardest thing would be on what she would be telling Trudy parents about what happened to her. This alone made Sharon very unhappy, for she would be the one facing Trudy's parents. They broke down with sadness. That's when a great tug came on the boat. It was Darius climbing onto the boat, holding the last bit of the potion that Elder Nadia gave him for a peace offering before the battle began. But before Jordon jumped up and transformed into a battle wolf, Darius waved the potion into Jordon's face, saying not to harm him, for he would release the last drop of liquid on the boat and harm everyone on the boat. Because Sharon was not immortal, she would feel the potion the worst if Darius released it onto the boat, and Jordon just couldn't take that chance. Darius raised up his paw and bowed his head while saying, "He comes in peace and wishes not to come in war, for he is wounded and wishes not to do no harm to no one. He started saying that he was an outcast to his pack, and they were out looking for him to do harm to him. Then he continued, saying that he wanted to go to the new world to start a new life with the pack over there and would do no harm to anyone anymore but to live out the remaining part of his life with a pack that knew nothing about violence and to live in peace. But what Darius really had in mind was he wanted to raise up a new army to return back to the Maypop Mountain with the largest army and wage war with Elder Nadia to take all the magic from her hands of.

That's when the water turned rapid as they reach the entrance to take them to the new generation. Traveling now through a vertex, the things surrounding them started shape-shifting, and only Sharon mind was wondering in away her memory of the Maypop Mountain became vivid. When Darius was traveling through the tunnel, his wounds started to heal themselves, and his body size became smaller. His fur became finer, while the mountain took Jordon's power from him. As Jordon well sculpt body with the dark tattoo disappearing from his muscular frame. The shine from his gold-plated trim also disappeared from his skin. But Elder Nadia made sure that he kept his strength, just in case he would need to protect himself from any danger that might come to him in the new world and coming back to the mountain. They were now tossed out of the boat caused by the bad current. They now struggled to reach the side of the river with Ricky in their sight, sitting on a falling tree, not knowing that they had arrive. Once Ricky looked up and saw that there were people with an animal coming out of the water, wet, he realized that one of them was Sharon. Screaming out to her to let her know that he was here for her and ready to help, he realized that Trudy wasn't with them. They were tired from struggling to stay afloat and trying to gain the strength to walk out of the water and place herself on to a falling tree. She caught her breath before telling Ricky who was accommodating her, and the dog wasn't a dog but a wolf! Darius, unable to talk or communicate for the magical privilege the mountain gave to those who lives on it.

Jordon did not realize this six-foot tall gentleman walked out of the water, as if the water didn't affect him at all. This man stood in front of Ricky and greeted himself as he would if he was on the Maypop Mountain. Ricky unable to speak while admiring the size of Jordon. Jordon introduced himself to Ricky with a heavy voice of royalty, asking Ricky if there was anything he could do to help with making a fire to warm Sharon up from the coldness of the water. As for Darius, he just walked up and down the river, trying desperate to gain his voice back to talk with the new wolves to win control over the local wolf pack. After Ricky was greeted by Jordon, he looked at Sharon and asked about Trudy as he prepared himself for some bad news. But when Sharon told him all that happened of what little she remembered, they then stared on their way back to the town to where they could catch a ride to the airport. Walking seemly for hours, Sharon was still filling Ricky with magic stories of this new

Eden. Still puzzled by all of this but only to think of some of the things have to have truth to this because there, standing in front of him, here two unexplained creatures, so something had to be true.

Now, while Jordon walked alongside Sharon, he couldn't help but to notice how the plants weren't look healthy as they were on the mountain. And the animals were not traveling in groups nor looking healthy too! As he continued to travel with the group through the woods, they came past of what look like an old house that no one had lived for centuries covered all over with forest. Just then, Jordon remembered when he was a little boy, and the family was escaping from the plantation, hiding in the woods. They too came to this home, where someone was living there at that time, helped them with food and water, and told his uncle the directions to the mountain. Now Jordon was so surprised that he remembered all of this.

Darius, now with no voice but only sounds, had to rethink of taking over the new world. Powerless and no pack that he could run with, he started to feel helpless. So Darius decided to keep close to gain friendship with Jordon to keep him safe until they returned to Maypop Mountain. But with the new knowledge of the new world, he would develop new skills and knowledge once he returned to the mountain. He realized for the first time that he felt lonely of not having a family with little ones running around him for protection and a girl wolf standing beside him with love in her eyes for him. So busy trying to destroy a family from the mountain, Darius did realize that he didn't have a family of his own.

Now coming to the end of the forest, Sharon, Jordon, Ricky, and the wolf Darius started to notice sounds of laugher and kids playing, coming in the direction of the town. Once they saw the little town, they all began to act and look presentable before the towns-people noticed them. Ricky started to fix his shirt. Sharon started to fix her hair, and Jordon and Darius tried to look friendly but found it difficult to do so because they had never seen anyone that were not from the mountain before. Jordon looked over and seen a shirt hanging on a branch and lucky was a little small but was enough to cover some of his trible makings so it would draw any attention to himself.

just making it to the town where everyone noticed their presence. From laughter and kids play came to a quick silence and only stares from the peoples of the town, not ever seeing anyone returning from those wood before and to see a very large shapely man and an oversized dog that was with them. That's when Ricky started to purchase may clothing for Jordon to help him blend in with the crowd. That's when Jordon noticed an older man stepping out of his porch to witness what the commotion was all about. Jordon remembered this man who once went fishing at the forbidden river. He watched this man for hours while standing in a thick wooden area across the river. This older gentleman was singing and fishing to catch dinner for his family. Just before the older man called it a day, he threw one last casting rod. He might have landed himself a large fish for his supper. As the man threw out his rod farther than he would normally do, one of the mountain fish traveled in the river area that they were not allowed to travel and got hooked by the older man's fishing line. In needing to save one of the mountain creatures, Jordon was curious on how this would play out. So the man felt something big on his fishing line. And with excitement, he gave all his strength in pulling this fish to the riverbank. When the old man realized this wasn't a normal fish from the river, he just stared at the fish in shock. This fish was very large than the average fish in this water, and it had pearlized, colorful scales on it. Knowing that people would never believe him of what he just caught, with excitement and great joy, he looked all around the riverbank to see what he could fine to help take this huge fish for everyone to see. But looking back at the giant fish, losing life for being out of the water for quite some time now, the old man had a change of heart, thinking, what if this was the only fish of its kind! This was the only proof that the myth about the Maypop Mountain did exist, and he was the first to bear witness. So with the excitement of meeting this fish, he threw the fish back into the river to save its life. The attention that the fish would have brought many people to their town and the gossip of him catching this fish would be the town talk for years to come. Then the old man would bring travelers from all over, nothing this quiet mountain and the old man just wanted to deal with that. So he decided that telling a story on how he caught a big rainbow fish to the locals would be all he needed in his life.

That's when Jordon walked up to this old man and said with only a few words, "I was there! And thank you!" Placing into the old man's hands a fish scale with pearlized colors on it, the old man just stared at it, not noticing that Jordon had walked off. Now the old man had proof of his rainbow fish–catching stories, not knowing that this fish scale close to his bed would grant him good dreams and wishes that would come true.

Jordon then knew now, with the help of Sharon, he would have a lot to offer these people as he learned the culture of many to take back to the Maypop Mountain to teach his people these new ways. That's when he felt a gentle touch on his back, and Jordon turned and looked over his shoulder to see an older lady touching him on his back. This lady introduced herself as a third generation of medical women and began to say that her great-grandmother always told them about a story her father told them about a magical mountain that you only have to be chosen by God. This mountain had so much power, not for every human to have. She also told Jordon about her great-aunt who escaped from a plantation and was never heard from again and that it was always told that they were the blessed ones to make it over on the Maypop Mountain. By the looks of Jordon's unique tattoos, he would have some idea of what she was talking about.

Jordon reached in his pouch and pulled out a maypop flower and laid it in the lady's hand. Hearing about this flower her whole life but not never thinking that she would be holding one in her hand, with pure excitement of laying her eyes on the flower, she asked Jordon if the myth was true that if you blow on the flower, you would see a nation of people praising God! Then she started to blow on the flower. The flower started to light up with a soft glow. And it waved from side to side, symbolizing the healing of the nations with this flower. This lady just witnessed a once-in-a-lifetime for nominal moment in time. Now realizing this magic got in the wrong hands would not come out good for the Maypop Mountain. So right at that moment, she looked up at Jordon and told him that it would stay a secret, and the medicine from this flower would be only to heal the sick. The lady also asked Jordon just before he walked off about her great-grandmother's sister! He then turned once again and said, "That's who told me to give you the flower," and then he turned and grab Sharon's hand and walked to the cab that was waiting for them.

About the Author

I am a first-time author. My love for learning and all the things I've experienced in this lifetime motivated me to start writing. I recently lost my mom in 2020, which was a great storyteller. Sitting and listening to her speak about how life was back in her era and how black poverty came to life during hard times has always sparked my interest. I've always seen things in a different perspective than others. Telling stories to me has always been a way to bond in my family, stories that have been passed down for years and still can help the younger generation. Rather the story is being told through singing, cooking, laughing, crying, playing spades. Like my great late mother, Betty Jean would say, "I remember back in my day..." and we all knew then, a *great* story was about to be told that we all can hold on to and tell today, stories that could and might just help someone else.